ICHABOD TOWARD HOME

ICHABOD TOWARD HOME

The Journey of God's Glory

WALTER BRUEGGEMANN

William B. Eerdmans Publishing Company
Grand Rapids, Michigan / Cambridge, U.K.

© 2002 Wm. B. Eerdmans Publishing Co.
All rights reserved

Wm. B. Eerdmans Publishing Co.
255 Jefferson Ave. S.E., Grand Rapids, Michigan 49503 /
P.O. Box 163, Cambridge CB3 9PU U.K.

Printed in the United States of America

06 05 04 03 02   7 6 5 4 3 2 1

Library of Congress Cataloging-in-Publication Data

Brueggemann, Walter.
Ichabod toward home: the journey of God's glory / Walter Brueggemann.
p.   cm.
Includes bibliographical references.
ISBN 0-8028-3930-4 (pbk.: alk. paper)
1. Bible. O.T. Samuel, 1st, IV-VI — Criticism, interpretation, etc.
I. Title.

BS1325.52.B78   2002
222'.4306 — dc21
2001058452

www.eerdmans.com

For
Kathleen M. O'Connor

Contents

Preface

These chapters are material that I presented as the Stone Lectures at Princeton Theological Seminary in February 2001. It is my intention in these chapters to exposit some themes which my *Theology of the Old Testament* in 1997 had anticipated. During the lectures I greatly enjoyed the hospitality of President Thomas Gillespie and especially the generosity of Professor and Mrs. Patrick Miller.

The manuscript reaches completed form through the patient wizardry of Tempie Alexander, to whom I express my boundless thanks. I am pleased to dedicate the book to my colleague Kathleen M. O'Connor with thanks for her patient, good-humored, generative collegiality. It is fitting that my lectures at Princeton Seminary, her alma mater, are offered in appreciation to her.

WALTER BRUEGGEMANN
Columbia Theological Seminary
Ash Wednesday, 2001

Abbreviations

AB	Anchor Bible
ABD	*The Anchor Bible Dictionary*, ed. David Noel Freedman
BibInt	*Biblical Interpretation*
BJS	Brown Judaic Studies
BZ	*Biblische Zeitschrift*
CBQ	*Catholic Biblical Quarterly*
EvT	*Evangelische Theologie*
HSM	Harvard Semitic Monographs
Int	*Interpretation*
JR	*Journal of Religion*
JSOTSup	Journal for the Study of the Old Testament Supplement
NRSV	New Revised Standard Version
OtSt	Oudtestamentische Studiën
SBLDS	SBL Dissertation Series
SJT	*Scottish Journal of Theology*
VTSup	Supplements to *Vetus Testamentum*
ZAW	*Zeitschrift für die alttestamentliche Wissenschaft*

(I)CHABOD DEPARTED

The question of what the church is doing and is to do when it stands before a biblical text is a complicated, contested, and endlessly important
question. It is a perennial and recurring question, the answer to which has
some constant contours. At the same time, however, the question evokes
and requires different nuances of response in different contexts. There is
no doubt that the question is a peculiarly urgent one in our church setting
in the West — given the seismic transformations in Western culture, the
complete reformulation of socio-economic relations in the face of new
technologies, and the pressures, threats, and opportunities of the new
globalism and its consequent pluralism.

In these lectures I will seek to respond to that question, not because I
think I can give anything like a satisfying answer, but because I believe that
a company like this has no more important work than to struggle together
with that endlessly contested issue. I understand that the question finally
receives its serious answer not in such reflective venues as this, but in the
actual practice of the church as it takes up matters of missional obedience.
But then, this company is more or less a form of the church asking about
missional obedience. And therefore the issue is a proper one even in this
venue.

In the first three lectures I will reflect at some length on the particular
text of 1 Samuel 4–6, conventionally termed "the Ark narrative."[1] I have

---

1. See Leonhard Rost, *The Succession to the Throne of David* (Sheffield: Almond, 1982),
6-34; Antony F. Campbell, *The Ark Narrative.* SBL Dissertation Series 16 (Missoula:
Scholars, 1975); and Patrick D. Miller, Jr., and J. J. M. Roberts, *The Hand of the Lord: A Reas-*

1

chosen this text not quite at random. I trust that my reason for settling on this text will in the end become clear to you. I will reflect critically in my two final lectures upon my exposition of the Ark narrative with attention to the question, what the church does and is to do when it stands before a biblical text.

I

The first sweeping move of this narrative in 1 Samuel 4 is Israel's *descent into loss*. The purported reportage invites the listening community gathered around the text into deep loss. The narrative moves, sentence by sentence, deep into loss, clear to the bottom of loss, as far as the narrator is able to imagine loss. The narrative serves to line out the remembered loss of the listening congregation in every new hearing of experienced loss, to name and give form to loss that may be deeply felt but nonetheless inchoate. Beyond that, moreover, the narrative summons the texted community even beyond its own loss to a more primordial loss that is available only in the studied, daring imagination of the narrative. Thus I take up the beginning of the so-called Ark narrative to consider the ways in which the text — and its reiterated telling in the church — provides an expression of extremity, a "limit expression," in order to give access to bewildered grief at the limit that is beyond the reach of either critical analysis or reasonable explanation.[2]

The tale of loss, if we accept the critical judgment of Patrick D. Miller and J. J. M. Roberts, is already voiced and underway in 1 Samuel 2.[3] Against the older critical consensus going back to Leonhard Rost, Miller and Roberts include 1 Sam. 2:12-17, 22-25, 27-36 as an introduction to that particular narrative. These earlier verses focus on the failures of the priest Eli and the affronts of his sons; they declare that Hophni and Phinehas must die. And with them the priestly house of Eli must be terminated.

The judgment brought by the narrative against the sons, partly voiced

---

sessment of the *"Ark Narrative" of I Samuel* (Baltimore: Johns Hopkins University Press, 1977).

2. On the phrase "limit expression," to be understood in relation to "limit experience," see Paul Ricoeur, "Biblical Hermeneutics," *Semeia* 4 (1975): 107-45.

3. Miller and Roberts, 27-31 and *passim*.

by their father, is a classic formulation of a prophetic speech of judgment.[4] The *indictment* against the sons is that "they had no regard for the Lord or for the duties of the priests to the people" (2:12-13). This disregard was expressed as an exploitative self-indulgence concerning meat brought for sacrifices to the Lord, a sin that is "very great in the eyes of the Lord" (2:17). This exploitative economic act is matched, not surprisingly, by sexual misconduct: "They lay with the women who served at the entrance to the tent of meeting" (2:22). The violations of money and sexuality characteristically come together. For this affront Eli rebukes his sons, but they would not listen. Thus verses 12-17, 22-25 voice the indictment.

The *sentence* against them, given in the next paragraph, is sweeping and uncompromising:

> See, a time is coming when I will cut off your strength and the strength of your ancestor's family, so that no one in your family will live to old age. Then in distress you will look with greedy eye on all the prosperity that shall be bestowed upon Israel; and no one in your family shall ever live to old age. . . . The fate of your two sons, Hophni and Phinehas, shall be the sign to you — both of them shall die on the same day. (2:31-32, 34)

The most remarkable feature of this sentence of termination is that it is played against the former unconditional promise that YHWH had made to this house:

> I promised that your family and the family of your ancestor should go in and out before me forever. (2:30)

The conduct of the sons is so outrageous, however, that even this unconditional promise previously voiced by YHWH to Eli must now be voided. The voiding of an unconditional promise of YHWH of course is an extremity. The pattern of indictment and sentence is clear and complete. We are only to await the enactment of the judgment with its loss that is sure to follow in the narrative.

---

4. The standard study of the genre is by Claus Westermann, *Basic Forms of Prophetic Speech* (Philadelphia: Westminster, 1967).

The sentence is reiterated in the following chapter, in the very different account of the dream-oracle of the boy Samuel:

On that day I will fulfill against Eli all that I have spoken concerning his house, from beginning to end. For I have told him that I am about to punish his house forever, for the iniquity that he knew, because his sons were blaspheming God, and he did not restrain them. Therefore I swear to the house of Eli that the iniquity of Eli's house shall not be expiated by sacrifice or offering forever. (3:12-14)

The Ark narrative continues in 4:1-2 with an implementation of the judgment. Israel is at war with the Philistines . . . of course. Israel is at war, theologically construed, in order to maintain its distinctive identity as YHWH's people in the land. The report is terse. Israel was defeated by the Philistines; about 4000 Israelites were slaughtered. The narrative does not explicitly connect the defeat to the preceding; if, however, we move from chapter 2, then this defeat is a rather inexact, clumsy implementation of the severe sentence against the priestly house. The sons of Eli are not mentioned in this battle report; but many Israelites were slain.

I linger over this brief introductory battle report only to notice that it is conventional and needs no particular comment. It reports loss that is, with chapter 2, completely contained in a prophetic lawsuit; the historical sweep of defeat is well placed by the narrative as punishment for guilt:

The sin. . . was very great in the eyes of the Lord. (2:17)

If someone sins against the Lord, who can make intercession? (2:25)

No one in your family will live to old age. (2:31)

The iniquity of the house of Eli shall not be expiated by sacrifice. (3:14)

Loss well placed under the rubric of guilt constitutes no severe theological problem for Israel and not much of a burdensome pastoral dilemma. Loss situated in trusted moral coherence is bearable and credible. No problem so far, except a few "acceptable deaths." These few "acceptable deaths" push to no extremity and do not evoke wonderments about theodicy.

II

But of course the narrative is now only at its beginning. Now Israel, according to the narrative, moves beyond the symmetrical calculus of covenant. The Israelites, routed and bewildered in their defeat, make a second effort against the Philistines (4:3-11). They bring the ark of the covenant into the battle camp, the ark upon which sits the invisible deity in whom Israel has complete confidence. The stakes are upped considerably by the palpable presence of YHWH, as the narrative now moves beyond the rubric of guilt. As the ark is introduced — into the camp and into the narrative — the narrative takes pains to identify this fresh initiative that piles up self-conscious theological phrasing:

> Let us bring *the ark of the covenant* of the Lord here from Shiloh, so that he may come among us and save us from the power of our enemies. So the people sent to Shiloh, and brought from there the ark of the covenant of *the Lord of hosts,* who is *enthroned on the cherubim.* (4:3b-4a)[5]

The ark is now present, and its purpose is to "save" *(yš')* from the hand of the enemy (4:3). The specific focus on Eli's sons is now forgotten, with attention only on the Philistine threat to Israel. The narrative begins to move well beyond the scope of the oracle of judgment in the earlier chapters. The ark is welcomed into the Israelite camp with a mighty shout. The Israelites are buoyant, exuberant, and confident.

1. Israelite exuberance has its counterpoint in the Philistine response to the shout (4:7-9). The Philistines promptly learn that the ark is the occasion of the Israelite shout. The Philistines, well schooled in Israelite history and theology, respond in fear, as well they might. The Philistines, in this narrative, as David Jobling has shown, are the totally, threatening, unclean "other."[6] They embody everything that contradicts and negates Israel and the God of Israel. They may be a historical enemy, but we should not miss that they are the paradigmatic enemy that seeks to live life outside the

---

5. For a review of the divine names in their several formulations, see Tryggve N. D. Mettinger, *In Search of God: The Meaning and Message of the Everlasting Names* (Philadelphia: Fortress, 1988).

6. David Jobling, *1 Samuel.* Berit Olam (Collegeville: Liturgical, 1998), 197-243.

covenantal realities of Israel, an "otherness" signified by a lack of circumcision. In their otherness, they constitute deep challenge and threat to Israel.

Here, in their alienness, the Philistines perform an odd role to contribute to Israelite exuberance. First, they know, as well as any Israelite, the Exodus story. They may have read Torah or perhaps have observed a Passover. They know that the "gods of Israel" have defeated the mighty power of Egypt. They know that the exodus was a God-given reversal of political power; they themselves, moreover, become candidates for slavery if they, like Egypt, are defeated by YHWH. And so, second, they cry out in their fear, "woe . . . woe," a short-term phrase that alludes to the dread of death. The Philistines know that the God of life, the Lord of the exodus, takes no prisoners, but destroys all those who resist the new sovereignty. The Philistines are the paradigmatic resisters now under threat. The God of Israel will eliminate "the other." The Philistines in response, however, do not wilt but brace for battle. The Philistines' appearance serves to enhance the God of Israel and to lead us to expect that the defeat of Israel in 4:1-2 will be reversed in Israel's favor.

2. But now, the narrative report takes a curious turn (4:10-11). The battle is joined. Israel is defeated. The Israelites flee home out of the reach of the Philistines. Thirty thousand died, dwarfing the figure of 4000 in the first encounter. If this is judgment against Eli's house, it is blatantly disproportionate and unbearably extreme. The battle report of 4:10-11 is not yet finished. It concludes with the final report we have anticipated: "the two sons of Eli, Hophni and Phinehas, died." That was to be expected; the enactment of the oracle of judgment against the house of Eli is complete.

But the penultimate scene of the report is stunning: "The ark of God was captured!" (4:11). This turn of affairs is completely unanticipated, not signalled by anything heretofore in the text. It is surely unanticipated by the exuberant Israelites. It is equally unanticipated by the frightened Philistines. We are not told, but apparently the defeat was quite unanticipated as well by the God of the covenant who must have taken the Philistines to be an easy mark after the Egyptians. The narrative, in verse 11, nicely joins these two outcomes that refuse to be joined. Concerning *Hophni and Phinehas*, the outcome is expected and fits the taxonomy of guilt. The capture of *the ark*, however, is well beyond any such calculus. Now the story moves completely out of the grid of guilt.

For the remainder of the chapter we are kept aware of the fate of *the house of Eli*. The judgment on the priestly house is complete. The surplus, however, concerns *the ark*. The two themes remain twinned, *priesthood* subordinated to *ark*.

- The report is given to the old man Eli who has heard and wondered about the cry now on the lips of Israel:

  Your two sons also, Hophni and Phinehas, are dead, and the ark of God has been captured. (4:17)

Eli's response to the loss of the ark is of course astonishment. He fell over, broke his neck, and died. The text says his response was not to the death of his sons which he expected. It was his response to the fate of the ark, a fate beyond his imagining. He died. He was, we are told, *heavy!* (*Kabod;* 4:18).

- The same news was told to Eli's unnamed daughter-in-law, wife of Phinehas. She also learned of the double failure, death to her husband and father-in-law, capture of the ark. And then she gave birth. Her labor pains were overwhelming. The father-in-law, upon hearing the news, came to death. The daughter-in-law, upon hearing the same news, came to birth. Both were pushed to extremity, one to death, one to birth, both pushed out of the ordinary by news for which they had no categories of reception or understanding.

The narrative is insistent and does not want us to miss the main point:

- The report: "The ark of God was captured." (4:11)
- The report to Eli: "The ark of God has been captured." (4:17)
- The report to the daughter-in-law:

  "The ark of God was captured." (4:19)

- The response of the daughter-in-law in extremity, because

  "The ark of God had been captured." (4:21)

- The narrator explains, at the end of the chapter, her extreme response, because

  "The ark of God has been captured." (4:22)

Five times, "the ark of God has been captured." There is no mistake and no denial: the ark of God has been captured!

7

This devastation has nothing to do with earlier judgment against the house of Eli. There has been, in mobilization against the Philistines, a gross miscalculation. The Israelites in their joy never doubted the efficacy of YHWH's ark. The Philistines matched Israelite joy with their own fear; they also did not doubt. YHWH, on the ark, has moved boldly into the field of combat. But then, comes wholesale slaughter. We are given a quick, wild battle scene, strewn with bodies, frantic, escaping soldiers, blood, and crying. In the midst of it all is the ark, taken by the Philistines as a trophy. It is a moment of loss well beyond guilt. It is indeed a moment of loss beyond faith. It is a moment of loss that defies theological coherence, a loss underneath all losses. The loss invites the unthinkable, that YHWH could not manage, did not prevail, was not strong enough, did not care enough, could not cope. Miller and Roberts say it well enough:

> Yahweh, represented in the form of the ark, seems to have bowed to the superior might of the Philistines' gods . . . the abandonment by Yahweh of his people in recognition of that superiority [of Dagon].[7]

Everything has come to an end. It was no final loss in Israel for the priestly house to go under. But now Israel's point of reference, Israel's raison d'etre in the world, is all gone.

3. The nameless daughter-in-law voices the loss (4:21). Her women companions try to reassure her in this liminal moment when the baby is born and the mother dies; but "she did not answer or give heed" (v. 20). What she sensed of loss outdistanced their assurance. Her last gasp was for naming the child, a moment of desperate awareness and acknowledgment. She would not be talked out of her pathos-filled truth-telling by their assurances. She called the new baby "Iy-kabod," that is, "Where is the glory?" The familiar translations of the name give answer to the question; but in fact she only asks the question in the name, "Where?" The answer, given in the next clause, is "Nowhere! Not here. . . . The glory is gone!"

This is an extraordinary piece of theology by this dying, unnamed daughter-in-law. She has grasped the point of the capture of the ark and its nearly unutterable significance. After the accent on "save" in verse 3, we might have expected her to say that YHWH's capacity to save has gone. But

7. Miller and Roberts, 42-43.

no, she says "glory." She understands that the issue is not *Israel's* future, but *YHWH's* own loss. It is YHWH who has been shamed and humiliated, and who has lost credence. She is, moreover, a better Yahwistic theologian than the Philistines, for the Philistines had thought like generic theologians and had assumed that YHWH, like every God, goes from victory to victory. But the daughter-in-law knows that this God is exposed and vulnerable, not generically sovereign, but vulnerable to the vagaries of historical challenge. She ponders the deep disruption in the very character of YHWH, the one completely at risk in the risk of Israel.

Her use of the term *kabod* is astonishing. If we can at all date texts, she is among the first to use it. Later on, the term will be a way of speaking of YHWH's *power and splendor* as a mighty force (see Exod. 14:4, 17-18; Isa. 4:5; Ezek. 28:22; 39:13). But not yet. Later on, the term would be a way of speaking of solemn, *sure cultic presence* as in Exod. 40:34; Lev. 9:6, 23; Num. 14:10. But not yet. Not yet made familiar currency by professional theologians. Before the theologians could do their work, here the term sits on the lips of this nameless woman. She uses this word so freighted with awe, splendor, majesty, and sovereignty only in order to negate. Not any of that . . . only loss that is inscrutable . . . only loss that drops the bottom out of Israel's buoyancy and gives the lie to Philistine fear. The glory of YHWH was to cohere and guarantee and assure. Now it has failed . . . now only a dead husband, a dead father-in-law, a routed army, a field of abandoned bodies, all topped by a humiliated God become an enemy trophy. In her last moment she sees all this. She says "where" and she dies. And dying, she knows . . . not anywhere that matters.

4. She has yet one more surprise in her acumen. Our familiar phrasing of her justification of the odd name of the child is "the glory has departed." But that is not quite right. What she says is, "The glory has gone into exile *(glh)* from Israel . . . for it has been taken." Neither she in verse 21 nor the narrator in verse 22 bothers to identify the agent, "taken" by whom? Everyone knows. It is the Philistines . . . the uncircumcised, polluting Philistines, the unbearable "other" whose very presence pollutes and demeans. And now YHWH is helpless, leaving Israel void of succor or hope. YHWH is taken against YHWH's own will, under the power of another, a captured trophy. One can picture the ark and its invisible occupant, perhaps in a caged wagon, the God of Exodus looking wearily between the bars as the procession moves toward Ashdod; or not on a wagon, but staggering in despair in the long, humiliating walk to Dagon's shrine. The daughter-in-law

dies; her death in bodily ways matches the fate of Israel and the condition of Israel's God . . . humiliated, shamed, powerless, void of conventional claims, absent of the marks of splendor to which Israel had become accustomed in its God.

The narrative pauses before 5:1, perhaps because the trek from the battlefield of Ebenezer-Aphek to the shrine at Ashdod was too long. In any case, the Philistines were in no hurry, for they relished each triumphal step. Israel, by contrast, has spiraled down into loss . . . death and despair. The loss is not any longer aligned with Israel's guilt. This is not covenantal judgment, for in the preceding narrative YHWH has not offered any such massive condemnation to justify this drama. It is simply failure. The narrative requires a dying moment to speak the deathliness beyond every reason. The categories of morality which might explain have been superseded. Now there is only loss, shock, bewilderment, abandonment . . . and finally silence . . . silence all the way into the night, awaiting the dawn of chapter 5.

III

Now I have taken this long in reading this text — perhaps overreading — because I believe it to be one of the most powerful broodings about loss in the entire Old Testament. I believe, moreover, that the *full embrace of loss,* so characteristic in Israel's faith, is one of the most urgent and important tasks left to the church and its ministry in our society. I wish now to extrapolate in two directions from this narrative that culminates with the utterance of this stunningly perceptive unnamed, dying theologian. I will consider in turn extrapolations of an intertextual variety, within Israel's ancient canonical text. And second, I will make some forays beyond the scope of Israel's text.

My first extrapolation is to suggest that this narrative of loss is one access point into the larger field of *loss that preoccupies Israel.* That is, I wish to consider the canonical futures evoked by this text, while begging the question of whether this text is early. It is in any case clear that this text is not only about itself, as Israel's texts never are; it insists on making contact with other texts. The narrative invites reflection on the way in which this believing literature requires reference to other texts. I shall identify five of these other texts in order to locate our text.

1. There is no doubt that this text intends connections
narrative. Indeed as an anti-Exodus text, perhaps it is a c
about making too much of the exodus.[8] The narrativ_ ₁
Philistines to introduce the exodus theme:

> Who can deliver us from the power of these mighty gods? These are
> the gods who struck the Egyptians with every sort of plague in the
> wilderness. (4:8)

The Philistines know the credo news from Israel, perhaps having read
Gerhard von Rad. They know that YHWH "acts in history" and has been
powerful against established power. They fully anticipate that always and
everywhere, here and now, YHWH will replicate that wonder of the exodus. The lips of the Philistines, the abhorrent other, mouth a doxology toward YHWH that is parallel to that of that other great unqualified outsider, Rahab (Josh. 2:9-13).

More than that, the Philistines are capable of connecting theology to
lived social reality:

> . . . in order not to become slaves to the Hebrews as they have been
> to you. (1 Sam. 4:9)

They understand that the splendor of YHWH has to do with social power
and economic relationships. They understand, moreover, that commensurate with a God who overturns power is a people who will subjugate others. The Philistines are here made to be an anticipation of the Marxian
awareness that "the criticism of religion is indeed the criticism of political
power." The Philistines expect — perhaps require — YHWH to be engaged
in the conventional contest of domination. This present narrative undermines an overreading of the Exodus narrative, as though Israelite faith is
always, everywhere, about winning. Exodus is not so readily replicated,
and this God is now seen to be more nuanced . . . and more vulnerable . . .
than a flat Exodus doxology might allow. The narrative, so to say, decons-
tructs the God of the exodus.

8. See William L. Moran, "The End of the Unholy War and the Anti-Exodus," in *A Song
of Power and the Power of Song: Essays on the Book of Deuteronomy,* ed. Duane L. Christensen
(Winona Lake: Eisenbrauns, 1993), 147-55.

2. The double use of *exile (glh)* in verses 21-22 inescapably must be taken as an allusion to 6th-century exile, surely the defining lived reality of Old Testament Israel.[9] There is now great uneasiness about the term "exile" among those scholars who do ideology-critique because, it is said, the term is not historically accurate but is a self-serving ideological mantra among a small party of elites.[10] Perhaps; but it is difficult to imagine this nameless woman among such elites. In any case, this narrative, now placed in the so-called Deuteronomic history, anticipates the ending of Israel's royal narrative in exile, knowing in its own primitive formulation all that is to befall Israel in time to come.

Whatever may be said about the term "exile," there is no serious doubt that there was a deep hiatus in the 6th century when Israel lost its temple, its monarchy, and all its conventional props and certitudes that had given dignity to its theological claims. "Exile" is that moment when the glory is gone, when Israel must learn to live without God in the world. The exile, here given in inchoate form, raised deep, abiding, and unanswerable questions for Israel that Israel must endlessly ponder:

- What have we done to warrant this? a question endlessly answered by the Deuteronomists and the prophets.
- How shall we live now in deep displacement?
- What now do we know about God,

    from whom our way is hid (Isa. 40:27),
    whose hand seems shortened (Isa. 50:2),
    who has forsaken and forgotten? (Isa. 49:14)

- How may we hope, or is this all there is?

These questions were a long time being formed in Israel, a longer time in being embraced, and yet a much longer time in being answered. The cir-

---

9. K. A. D. Smelik, "The Ark Narrative Reconsidered," *New Avenues in the Study of the Old Testament,* ed. A. S. van der Woode. OTS 25 (Leiden: Brill, 1989), 128-44, connected the Ark narrative to the exile and regards it as a parable of the Babylonian exile.

10. See the discussions of Hans M. Barstad, *The Myth of the Empty Land: A Study in the History and Archaeology of Judah During the "Exilic" Period* (Oslo: Scandinavian University Press, 1996); James M. Scott, ed., *Exile: Old Testament, Jewish, and Christian Conceptions* (Leiden: Brill, 1997); and Lester L. Grabbe, ed., *Leading Captivity Captive: "The Exile" as History and Ideology.* JSOTSup 278 (Sheffield: Sheffield Academic, 1998).

cumstance of departed glory generated competing interpretive traditions (sects), a vigorous kind of pluralism that would do battle for the future; the circumstance of exile evoked immense imaginative generativity in which Israel created its sacred corpus. From the evidence it is clear that this is a people candidly driven to its loss that has the energy and freedom to push to newness, an energy and freedom not yet given to those on the safe side of loss.

3. More specifically, the departure of glory surely alludes to or is taken up by Ezekiel, the prophet who attended most to YHWH's glory. By the time of Ezekiel, Israel had a well-developed theology of temple presence that is not on the horizon of the Ark narrative. By the time of Ezekiel, "glory" that had to do with leverage and contested power has been transposed into static presence, a presence celebrated in the tabernacle of Exodus 40, a visible, palpable sense of YHWH's in-dwelling, life-guaranteeing presence in the sanctuary.

But, of course, Ezekiel ponders that palpable, life-guaranteeing presence only to draw negative conclusions:[11]

- In chapter 8, the prophet is given a tour of the Jerusalem temple. He finds there such a compromised religious practice that neither he nor YHWH can tolerate it and he can scarcely speak about it. Ezekiel witnesses abominations and greater abominations and "still greater abominations" (vv. 13, 15). The inevitable conclusion in such violated presence is of course judgment:

    > Therefore I will act in wrath; my eye will not spare, nor will I have pity; and though they cry in my hearing with a loud voice, I will not listen to them. (Ezek. 8:18)

- In chapter 9, the judgment is to be implemented with the death of those who compromised. Two notations are important. First, exceptions are made for those who "sigh and groan" over what has happened (v. 4). Second, it is asserted that YHWH "has abandoned the land" (v. 9). The land is now bereft of the glory that has guaranteed life.

11. See Ralph W. Klein, *Ezekiel: The Prophet and His Message* (Columbia: University of South Carolina Press, 1988), esp. 52-71.

- In chapter 10, the abandonment of Jerusalem by YHWH is graphically articulated:

> Then the glory of the Lord rose up from the cherub to the threshold of the house; the house was filled with the cloud, and the court was full of the brightness of the glory of the Lord. The sound of the wings of the cherubim was heard as far as the outer court, like the voice of God Almighty when he speaks. (Ezek. 10:4-5)

YHWH has dramatically, physically, quite publicly left the city, the place of presence. YHWH cannot and will not stay where YHWH's glory is cheapened and mocked. And so the city is left absent. YHWH, moreover, is made into an exile, driven by YHWH's own people far away. In an important way, Ezekiel plays upon and exposits the theme of the Ark narrative. The glory has indeed departed. At the same time, we may be instructed by the important contrast between these two dramas of departure. In the Ark narrative YHWH is weak and overwhelmed, left vulnerable to the greater power of Dagon. Of course that great Calvinist, Ezekiel, could never countenance weakness on the part of YHWH, so that with him, it is YHWH's initiative to depart, not to be denied glory but to give it up.

Ezekiel's statement of the initiative of YHWH nonetheless permits us to raise the question: Why was YHWH in the Ark narrative so vulnerable to capture? The answer surely must be that Israel's sins did not adequately serve and honor, and where Israel's adherence to YHWH is diminished, YHWH's glory is by that much diminished, until in the extremity of the Ark narrative YHWH is completely exposed in weakness. For whatever difference of nuance, our narrative sets out a theme of absence that comes to fruition in Ezekiel. In our narrative, the absence evokes the wretched final cry of the woman in labor. In Ezekiel the same absence reduces the prophet to muteness (Ezek. 24:25-27).[12] The prophet cannot speak as long as the absence prevails, as long as the glory is gone, as long as the city is exposed to death. Absence brings loss of voice and the shrinking of the capacity of the prophet.

4. Still on the theme of exile, linkages can be made between our narrative and the poetry of Lamentations. We have seen that the first defeat at

12. See Robert R. Wilson, "An Interpretation of Ezekiel's Dumbness," *VT* 22 (1972): 91-104.

the hands of the Philistines is surely punishment for guilty Israel (1 Sam. 4:1-2). But then we have seen, in the second defeat, a rout by the Philistines that includes the ark; the narrative moves beyond guilt and ends in a flood of grief, for "the ark of God was captured" (4:11). Guilt will explain the loss only up to a certain point. Indeed, the narrative is not so mesmerized by guilt as some interpreters incline.

The move from *guilt* to *grief* is not an easy one. It requires the move from an explainable symmetry to a depth of loss that resists any moralizing explanation. Defeat can be connected to the sons of Eli; but the capture of the ark admits no such linkage and ends in grief. The same move is evident in Lam. 3:40-66 concerning the loss of the city. There is no doubt that at first glance the destruction of Jerusalem in 587 B.C.E. can be understood in the prophetic calculus of indictment and sentence, a point accented by the Deuteronomists. In Lamentations 3, moreover, the accent on guilt is not ducked:

> We have transgressed and rebelled,
> and you have not forgiven.
> You have wrapped yourself with anger and pursued us,
> killing without pity. (Lam. 3:42-43)

Guilt, however, is sustainable only so long. Very soon the dread depth of failure and absence moves dramatically from guilt to grief that includes no moral dimension. Thus by verse 49, the poet asserts:

> My eyes will flow without ceasing,
> without respite . . .
> My eyes cause me grief
> at the fate of all the young women in my city. (Lam. 3:49, 51)

The poet now situates Israel as helpless and innocent victim of enemies who assault "without cause" *(ḥnn):*

> Those who were my enemies *without cause*
> have hunted me like a bird;
> they flung me alive into a pit
> and hurled stones on me;
> water closed over my head;
> I said, "I am lost." (Lam. 3:52-54)

15

You have seen the wrong done to me, O Lord;
judge my cause.
You have seen all their malice,
all their plots against me. (Lam. 3:59-60)

This is the voice of loss that no longer offers moral justification, a sadness, a need, a reaching, a yearning that is down to the bottom and unreasonable, regressive beyond the norms of obedience.[13] That is the same move, is it not, made in our narrative. No longer any interest in Eli's sons, no longer any interest in justification or explanation, only the stark awareness that the loss has cut beneath prophetic calculus to God's own life, power, and glory. This is not any longer the vulnerable appealing to the reliable, but now all are vulnerable and bereft.

5. If we see the line that runs from our narrative via *Ezekiel* to the *exile* and to the book of *Lamentations*, surely we may move more generally from Lamentations to *lament and complaint*, the voice of desperation and loss. That voice is beyond confession, short on doxology, only enough speech left to sound loss, voice situated in absence, daring yet to speak to promised presence, promised but not now palpable or convincing:

I am distraught by the noise of the enemy,
because of the clamor of the wicked.
For they bring trouble upon me,
and in anger they cherish enmity against me.
My heart is in anguish within me,
the terrors of death have fallen upon me.
Fear and trembling come upon me,
and horror overwhelms me. (Ps. 55:2-5)

All day long they seek to injure my cause;
all their thoughts are against me for evil.
They stir up strife, they lurk,
they watch my steps. (Ps. 56:5-6a)

---

13. On the depth and regression of such grief, see Tod Linafelt, *Surviving Lamentations: Catastrophe, Lament, and Protest in the Afterlife of a Biblical Text* (Chicago: University of Chicago Press, 2000).

Even now they lie in wait for my life;
the mighty stir up strife against me.
For no transgression or sin of mine, O Lord,
for no fault of mine, they run and make ready. (Ps. 59:3-4)

These many prayers that live at the edge of the church's horizon are acknowledgments that the glory has departed. Israel knows unmistakably about departed glory as does every attentive, candid pastor.[14]

These protests are, in the end, acts of hope.[15] But it is hope that is regressive and not usually buoyant. It is hope that bargains, that withholds praise and seeks to leverage, that promises to thank, that intends to bear witness, but not yet, not soon, not until the glory acts to heal. It turns out, in the candor of Israel, that the Philistines and Dagon, the God of the Philistines, take many forms, generally "enemy," enemy enough to dominate, adversary enough to preempt the space of YHWH. And Israel is left with the voice of a shrieking woman, "Alas, alas, departed, gone, exiles. Where is Kabod?"

It is clear that this *narrative of loss* and exile in 1 Samuel 4 is a narrative that echoes everywhere in Israel's canon of faith. It reverberates because Israel is marked by candor and will not lie to itself or its neighbors about its life. Israel will not, moreover, pretend to its God or about its God or on behalf of its God.[16] But this narrative also resounds because this God is known in Israel to have a dimension of vulnerability not to be easily overcome by strident assertions of sovereignty. Imagine, God captured by the Philistines!

IV

Now this is an exercise in biblical theology in which I have tried to be text-specific and canonically alert. But of course the force of this narrative —

14. See Erhard Gerstenberger, "Der Klagende Mensch: Anmerkungen zu den Klagegattungen in Israel," in *Probleme biblischer Theologie: Gerhard von Rad zum 70. Geburtstag*, ed. Hans Walter Wolff (Munich: Chr. Kaiser, 1971), 64-72.

15. Concerning the pastoral practice of loss and hope, see Kenneth R. Mitchell and Herbert Anderson, *All Our Losses, All Our Griefs: Resources for Pastoral Care* (Philadelphia: Westminster, 1983).

16. For an example of such theological candor, see David R. Blumenthal, *Facing the Abusing God: A Theology of Protest* (Louisville: Westminster/John Knox, 1993).

certainly for us who heed it as authoritative but perhaps well beyond our confessional privilege — moves outside the book into the world. It insists that loss is real and deep, and it exhibits the conviction that *loss voiced* is essential to survival.[17] It insists on that always, a point belatedly received by the Jewish sensibility of Sigmund Freud, who understood about *voiced loss*.[18]

If we are to do biblical theology that matters, the book in its peculiar, distinctive, exacting cadences spills into the world. It is the work and privilege of those who trust this book to be able to line out the saving truth of this text without excessive effort at relevance, without overwrought efforts to connect to contemporaneity, because when the text is faithfully and freely available, it enables connections that need not be forced or imposed.

- Beyond the scope of Israel's own text, I have of course been speaking of *Friday* and have been outlining a "Theology of the Cross."[19] Friday is that day of the departure of glory and exile and absence, the day of breaking old certitudes and shattering old ways of control and privilege. Friday is the day of absence and abandonment out of which we Christians regularly say "and him crucified." It is not easy to linger the right amount of time on Friday, just as our narrative probably did not know how many verses to have in chapter 4 or how many times to reiterate "the ark of God is captured." The narrator decided on five such utterances.

---

17. It is for good reason that Tod Linafelt, *Surviving Lamentations*, links survival to the act of voiced loss. Without the voicing, the loss will devour. More generally, see Elaine Scarry, *The Body in Pain: The Making and Unmaking of the World* (Oxford: Oxford University Press, 1985); and Judith Lewis Hernon, *Trauma and Recovery: The Aftermath of Violence — From Domestic Abuse to Political Terror*, rev. ed. (New York: Basic Books, 1997).

18. The capacity of voicing to transform grief is an elemental insight and gift of the Jewish tradition so well grasped by Freud, even if this undoubted reality lacks any "reasonable" explanation. Without this crucial insight into speech as transformative action, we may have been left with only the reasonable "thought" of the more dominant Greek tradition. On the high cost for culture in repressing such voicing of loss and the antidote of speech as concerns cultural possibility, see John Murray Cuddihy, *The Ordeal of Civility: Freud, Marx, Lévi-Strauss, and the Jewish Struggle with Modernity* (1974, repr. Boston: Beacon, 1987).

19. For a contemporary articulation of the theme, see Douglas John Hall, *Lighten Our Darkness: Toward an Indigenous Theology of the Cross* (Philadelphia: Westminster, 1976).

18

Some in our tradition linger on Friday too long, and what we get is an endlessly suffering Jesus. But it is possible as well, in a "can-do" church subservient to a "can-do" society, that Friday is too awkward; as a consequence we quickly feature empty crosses and rush to Sunday and reduce the truth of this God to an Easter parade.[20] We hurry to get it said liturgically on Saturday night, eagerly not waiting, but letting Friday pass almost unnoticed.

The Israelites did not have the complexity of the Trinity to let the Son die while the Father presides, even though Jürgen Moltmann has famously said that on Friday, "The Fatherlessness of the Son is matched by the Sonlessness of the Father."[21] In the early Friday cadences of the Ark narrative, it is all of YHWH captured, all of the glory exiled, nothing in reserve, nothing held back, evidencing a God who is marked in all coming days by loss, marked in ways that persist.

- Beyond the scope of Israel's own text, there looms the *Shoah* that admits of no "explanation," surely an unintelligible break marked by absence, a sacrament of barbarism over our century.[22] We debate whether the holocaust is unique or not, and offer what we can of human moralism or reason. Or with Richard L. Rubenstein, we give up on a God who could not be more reliable;[23] or with David R. Blumenthal we notice the abusiveness enacted in the ovens, seemingly by God.[24] But none of this finally satisfies. We are left with the raw event, much like Friday, only more massive and in some ways more contemporary, evidence at Auschwitz and Dachau echoed in a thousand other brutalities. The world is, on occasion, without God, perhaps God unwilling to be present with the dying, perhaps God unable

---

20. The pressure and temptation to "cheat" on this Friday truth is evidenced in the practice of a local church during Holy Week in the Christian calendar. During the service of Tenebrae, one light was left on, thus compromising the liturgical enactment of all of the darkness of Friday, a compromise that undermined the entire enterprise.

21. Jürgen Moltmann, *The Crucified God: The Cross of Christ as the Foundation and Criticism of Christian Theology* (New York: Harper & Row, 1974), 243.

22. See the analysis and argument of Steven Katz, *The Holocaust in Historical Context: Ancient and Medieval Cases* 1 (Oxford: Oxford University Press, 1994).

23. Richard L. Rubenstein, *After Auschwitz: History, Theology, & Contemporary Judaism*, 2nd ed. (Baltimore: Johns Hopkins University Press, 1992).

24. Blumenthal, *Facing the Abusing God.*

to stand the stress and so departing, perhaps God shoved aside because the perpetrators could not bear to act in God's presence. In any case, this is loss clear to the bottom, loss without redeeming quality, loss without life-giving spirit, loss without ordering creator, the world on its own, shriveling to brutality, a brutality immediate, but leaving its wake seemingly forever, because brutality seems never to end.

- Beyond the scope of Israel's own text, it takes not much imagination to consider that the glory has departed, leaving the world no longer the way it used to be. Francis Fukuyama not withstanding, we are witnessing the unravelling of the human world as it was, the old sureties of power and the reservoirs of heritage and learning, the reliable empires and the trusted certitudes.[25] There are, of course, powerful yearnings in society, in empire, and in church to recover the old coherence, to go back to what was. Even voicing that yearning for a lost coherence, a voicing quite common among Presbyterians, is a fearful acknowledgment of loss. In the very voicing, we are scarcely able to fend off the costs that are so immediate and the fears that are so palpable, the need for more security, even while anxiety seems always to trump security . . . new security, newer anxiety. And God — the God of fidelity and sovereignty — is captured, exiled, absent, powerless. The absence is partly explained by guilt — ample guilt — deep patterns of exploitation, oppression, and slavery. Those admissions, however, do not in the end suffice, and so there is grief for a glory that has departed.

- Beyond the scope of Israel's text, the void comes closer. It comes close in public arenas for which the 1999 carnage at Columbine High School in Littleton, Colorado, may stand as epitome. For all our pushing and shoving and blaming and suing and wondering, Columbine should not have happened, not raw violence committed against beloved children in privileged, secure suburbia. A failure of community fabric, an inattentiveness in family, a kind of crazy youth culture, a need for more generous public policy, for better gun control, for more vigilant police . . . whatever. The glory has departed from that place and many other places like it. There are, of course, efforts to recover and restore, but the scar of absence will persist.

---

25. Francis Fukuyama, *The End of History and the Last Man* (New York: Free Press, 1992). Fukuyama makes very curious reading when done in the context of Holocaust reportage.

- Beyond the scope of Israel's text, most of us do not have occasion — happily do not have occasion — for holocaust or for "the failure of the West," or even for Columbine. Nonetheless, the life of the church — and the work of the pastor — is saturated with loss. And when the immediacy of loss hits, it is as stubborn as "the failure of the West," as immediately unbearable as the Shoah, as dread-filled as Columbine, even if not as massive and visible. You know the list:

> Gene's nonsmoker's lung cancer;
> Barbara's malignancy;
> little Michael;
> Tim's forced departure from the parish;
> the vanished child;
> the paralyzed athlete;
> the lost job.

It comes, as the pastor knows, as the "Null Point," the zero hour, the shut down.[26] The pastor is called. The pastor is called because the pastor is "the Friday person" even in a secularized community, the one with the text and its candid cadences of loss that go clear to the bottom. It needs to be said and acknowledged, too many times, "the glory has departed." Such a truth that needs to be voiced, moreover, could not be made up on the spot. It is too heavy and too dangerous, too much beyond our management to be made up on the spot. That loss is to be lined out, rather, from mothers and fathers who have always known that truth since that Friday in Ashdod, when the truth was lined out five unflinching times. It is a lining out nobody wants to hear and nobody wants to say. Except that the integrity of faith and the candor lived life, not to say the integrity of the book, require it to be said: "The ark of God has been captured" . . . five times. . . . "The glory has departed."

---

26. I take the phrasing, "null point," from Walther Zimmerli, "Plans for Rebuilding After the Catastrophe of 587," *I Am Yahweh* (Atlanta: John Knox, 1982), 111, 115, 133. See derivatively, Walter Brueggemann, "Faith at the *Nullpunkt*," in *The End of the World and the Ends of God*, ed. John Polkinghorne and Michael Welker (Harrisburg: Trinity, 2000), 143-54.

V

This is an exercise in biblical theology. But the doing of biblical theology must needs be, characteristically, an exercise in social criticism. It must needs be so, because Israel always understood that the God it named and trusted was deep set in the fabric of daily life and not elsewhere. The truth needs to be said about *exiled glory* in order to live where God has placed us. Short of an affirmation of *glory exiled*, we too easily practice a "theology of glory" that uncritically celebrates too much. We do not put it as "theology of glory" of course, since we are not so intimate with Luther's phrasing. We do better to call it *denial*, the pretense that the absence does not reach to the bottom, that the point to which we come is not quite "null."

It strikes us that the Ark narrative tells the truth about YHWH. It refuses to explain everything in terms of guilt, because the loss has broken well beyond any thinkable guilt. Nor does it pretend that YHWH has prevailed against the Philistines. Indeed, if YHWH had wanted to prevail anywhere, it was surely against the Philistines. Against such a primal yen on YHWH's part to prevail over the Philistines, the narrative acknowledges YHWH's vulnerability in the face of Dagon's superior power. The narrative does not flinch from facing the truth about glory exiled, an exile YHWH could not resist, an exile of YHWH that foreshadows the deep inheritance of exile that will mark the people of YHWH.[27]

This is an exceedingly difficult theological claim. It is equally a difficult socio-economic, political, psychological claim. It is such a difficult claim that we devise ways to avoid.[28] Against such devising, I propose that in the doing of biblical theology in our time and place so bent on denial, the telling of truth about absence is not only difficult but so urgent.

It is urgent because:

---

27. As concerns the ongoing reality of exile in Jewish tradition and experience, see the eloquent and inescapable articulation of André Neher, *The Exile of the Word: From the Silence of the Bible to the Silence of Auschwitz* (Philadelphia: Jewish Publication Society of America, 1981).

28. There are, of course, countless ways to avoid. See Walter Brueggemann, "Texts That Linger, Not Yet Overcome," in *Shall Not the Judge of All the Earth Do What Is Right? Studies on the Nature of God in Tribute to James L. Crenshaw*, ed. David Penchansky and Paul L. Redditt (Winona Lake: Eisenbrauns, 2000), 21-41.

- A society ordered by denial is a society that cannot be richly human.
- A society ordered by denial is likely committed to *violence,* for what it cannot have genuinely and gracefully, it will have by force. It assumes that no violence will drive the glory away that is permanently present; such a supposedly guaranteed glory invites shamelessness.[29]
- A society ordered by denial is likely committed to *greed,* for it seeks to fill the void of candor by unembarrassed acquisitiveness, always at the expense of the neighbor who is scarcely noticed.
- A society ordered by denial is likely committed to *killing moralism,* because one way to fend off anxiety is to expel, silence, and imprison the dissenters. Denial requires the exclusion of the other.

Israel itself engaged, here and there, in denial. And in doing so, Israel predictably became infested with *violence, greed,* and *killing moralism.* These fruits of denial, in disobedient Israel or in the contemporary world, do not let us be human, do not make us safe, do not bring joy. In that community of covenant, the fruits of denial did not let Israel be fully Israel. As our narrative testifies, it is the odd vocation of this texted-community, in such a matrix of denial that is wide and deep, to be truth-telling, all the way down. Many of us lack courage for such truth-telling; but we take heart and substance from this ancient account of our mothers and fathers who managed to get it said five times in this text, "The ark of God has been captured."

---

29. On the loss of shame, see Abraham J. Heschel, *Who is Man?* (Stanford: Stanford University Press, 1965), 112-19.

JOY COMES IN THE MORNING

The last gasp of the unnamed daughter-in-law at the end of 1 Samuel 4 is a final statement of wretchedness, as narratively final as can be imagined. The outcome of that narrative leaves all in wretchedness. . . . Eli's family, Israel, the ark, and, we may believe, the God of the ark. It is a dismal way to end a chapter in the life of this God and in the book of this people. Perhaps it occurred to you from my first presentation, that it is also a dismal way to end a lecture. But that is how it was when the sun went down on Friday night in Ashdod.

I

The narrative, of course, does not end with chapter 4, or we would not be here doing what we are doing with this text. The narrative turns abruptly in chapter 5. But not before 5:1 reiterates and intensifies the wretchedness of chapter 4. The first verse of chapter 5 reiterates and intensifies in the way a teacher, bent on continuity, might quickly recall the substance of the last lecture, a substance usually forgotten by everyone else except the teacher. Indeed, we might imagine that Israel would have a difficult time with chapter 4 and might want to forget it at the first opportunity.

For whatever reason, 5:1 completes the drama of dismay of chapter 4:

When the Philistines captured the ark of God, they brought it from Ebenezer to Ashdod.

25

The battle is over and Israel has been routed; the Philistines have prevailed. The battle is over and YHWH has lost; Dagon has prevailed. The confrontation was at Ebenezer. The reference to that place is perhaps ironic, for it means "stone of help." From an Israelite perspective, perhaps the place should have been dubbed Eben-lo-Ezer, "stone of no help at all." No help from YHWH, no help for Israel. This turn of affairs against the Philistines gives the lie to the lyric of Israel:

> Happy are those whose help is the God of Jacob,
> whose hope is the Lord their God,
> who made heaven and earth,
> the sea, and all that is in them;
> who keeps faith forever. (Ps. 146:5-6a)

The Israelites are precisely not happy, because the God of Jacob has been no help at all. The Philistines exult.

Characteristically they form a triumphal procession, moving the totem of victory from Ebenezer, that sadly misnamed place. That place should have been a joyously freighted Israelite place, but alas, it was not. The Philistines move the evidence of victory to Ashdod, core habitat of Dagon. The Philistines form a victory parade that features all the captured booty of war. YHWH is a prisoner of war put on exhibit. One can imagine the Philistines on the sidewalks of Ashdod cheering; YHWH on YHWH's ark caged, looking through the bars of the cage, utterly humiliated, now in Ashdod, far from home, far from governance, failed. The parade is military and political. In the ancient world, however, as in the contemporary world, such military action depends on the legitimacy of civil religion for *gravitas;* and so the victory parade ends in a religious act. The parade winds its way to the temple where the priests of Dagon wait to receive the victory, engaging in prayers of thanksgiving, escalating the victory from military combat to cosmic significance. The priests at the door of the temple receive the parade, accept the booty, and carefully bring the booty to the icon of Dagon, who may not be the "Divine Warrior," but who is good enough to prevail over Israel.[1] Perhaps in their version, the priests and people uttered the victory liturgy:

---

1. On the theme, see Patrick D. Miller, Jr., *The Divine Warrior in Early Israel.* HSM 5 (Cambridge, Mass.: Harvard University Press, 1973).

Lift up your heads, O gates!
and be lifted up, O ancient doors!
that the King of glory may come in.
Who is the King of Glory?
Dagon, strong and mighty,
Dagon mighty in battle . . .
he is the King of glory. (see Ps. 24:7-10)

The day is over as the parade ends and the service concludes. The military leadership returns to the officers' club for a banquet. The priests check the doors and windows of the shrine; they turn out the lights and go home. The management of such a great public pageant, as every pastor knows, is exhausting. There are so many details and so many unreliable people who can distort the entire enterprise. Now everyone has gone home . . . military, priests, crowd, finally even the verger. It is very quiet, perhaps dark, "for the lamp of Dagon had not yet gone out."[2] Perhaps there is an eeriness, as you may know, if you have been silently alone for a long period of darkness in a holy place that is pregnant with divine presence.

Now come hours and hours of darkness and quiet. No one said anything. No one did anything, for hours and hours. And then it is morning. As the day dawns, there is a return to the temple. The text says, ". . . the people of Ashdod." We might have expected the priests to begin their daily liturgical responsibilities. But perhaps the celebration continued into another day, so much to celebrate. In any case, when they arrived at the shrine . . . pause . . . shock . . . stunned . . . amazed . . . bewildered. Everything was changed. Everything was inverted. Dagon had been left the night before as celebrated and preeminent and YHWH subservient. The liturgical arrangement reflected the imbalance of the battlefield of Ebenezer.

And now, Dagon has fallen on his face, the statue with its nose pressed to the floor. Where Dagon fell, there he lay. It was an accident, no doubt, merely a fall of stonework unbalanced. No, it was an act of obeisance; Dagon bowed deeply "before the ark of YHWH," having learned through the night, we know not how, that YHWH is the God before whom "every knee shall bow" and every nose shall be pressed low to the floor. All this time, YHWH never said a word, never made a gesture, never gloated, never smirched, never stared, just sat there passively and invisibly, worshipped by

2. I extrapolate from 1 Sam. 3:3.

27

the Philistine god who has been surreptitiously overcome in the night when there were no witnesses.

The Philistines who discover the dramatic inversion say nothing. Perhaps they are too shocked to speak. If they are priests, perhaps they hustle to get things "back in order" before people arrive, not realizing that things will never be "back in order." They do not want their constituency scandalized. Perhaps they think the collapse of Dagon is an accident. Or perhaps they know what this turn signifies. Perhaps they recognize at the edge of their awareness that the glorious victory of Dagon in chapter 4 has already come unglued. They never say a word in the text or give a hint of their thinking. It is all "perhaps," because the narrative is lean and restrained.

The Philistines act quickly. They restore Dagon to his permanent, upright place in the shrine; there he stays all day, victorious, receiving adulation yet again for the victory over Israel and over the God of Israel. Some surely celebrated in innocence as winners are wont to do, some perhaps suspecting otherwise as they noticed the peculiar scars on the stonework, some pretending because they may know otherwise, given the fact that already in chapter 4 the Philistines have been good theologians concerning the power of YHWH. And so the day passes. No doubt there were big crowds, soldiers bringing their families in awe at what has been so recently accomplished in the name of Dagon. Some sons in that patriarchal society thinking of glorious military service to come. Some — who have good, clear voices — thinking of a career in the priesthood, the glorious management of the great social emblems of victory. And then again comes the evening shutdown of the shrine, quiet, darkness, and all in stillness. A final check to make certain that Dagon is secure and in place, and then rest for all parties.

They did it all over again on the third day (5:4). They came again to the shrine. Some of the managers were perhaps by this time weary with crowd control. Some of the crowd were no doubt exuberant, because they had not been there the second day but had waited until the third day when the crowd would be somewhat less. They got an early start; they rose early on the third day. Again, shock, dismay, displacement, because the third day in the house of Dagon is like the second day, only more so. Again, Dagon has fallen, again with his nose pressed to the floor, either as crashed stonework fallen over or as a low bow before the silent, passive ark of YHWH. One cannot, however, on the third day simply reiterate the second day. There is more.

This time the head of Dagon's statue was cut off. The Philistine god had, in the night, lost his head, perhaps decapitated, or lost his head, gone

28

crazy, because trying to maintain preeminence in the presence of YHWH will drive one crazy. More than that, like Venus de Milo, Dagon's hands were cut off, his arms broken. The Philistine god has been effectively and decisively dis-armed, made weak, helpless, and impotent. This diminished Dagon, it is immediately clear, is no real Dagon, just a shell and charade who will never again triumph, never defeat, never win, never prevail. This is Dagon haplessly diminished. While the Philistines surveyed the sorry, inexplicable scene, the ark of YHWH never moved. YHWH never gestured, no wink, no notice, all is passive . . . and inexplicable. There the scene ends, abruptly.[3] This time, on the third day, the Philistines did not even try to reposition Dagon to a posture of power. The icon is now beyond restoration, feeble and discredited.

These verses are among the most graphic and awesome verses in all of Scripture. We may notice that the text is remarkably restrained. It does not explain, or even express curiosity or astonishment. It refuses to tell us anything. It passes quickly and silently over eight hours of darkness when whatever was to happen did happen. The narrative skips over the interesting parts because it does not know. The transformation and repositioning of the gods in the night happened without a witness. It is all "night-time work" when the skills, passions, and expertise of human agents are at rest, when the shadows are thick, the guard is down, and the ominous powers move to do their inscrutable work. All we see or know, all we ever see or ever know is the "before" and the "after." Our imagination, cynical or credulous, is required to fill in the 18 minutes of the erased tape or all eight hours of darkness unaccounted for. The narrator tells us a great deal. He steadfastly refuses, however, to tell us what we most want to know and finally must know.

II

The narrative, however, is not only restrained and laconic, refusing to tell us much. It is, to use Erich Auerbach's famous phrase, "fraught with background."[4] That is, not only is the hidden part not made visible by the narrator; the narrator suggests that we must pay attention to the dog that does

3. The scene of narrative action ends in verse 4, for verse 5 is of course an etiological comment.

4. Erich Auerbach, *Mimesis: The Representative of Reality in Western Literature* (Garden City: Doubleday, 1957), 9.

not bark, must notice the thickness between the lines, must pay attention in careful ways to what is said in its being left unsaid, offering only hints and traces. There is much more here than is uttered. And if missed, the narrative becomes a thin "miracle" to be dismissed as childish fantasy.

So let us reflect on that "fraught background." Partly we may imagine and fill in the gaps, as we regularly do. But partly we may see where, in Israel's recurring textual cadences, there are other utterances that assist us and illuminate our reading. In this case, I submit that these echoes that help us here are found in the exposé of the idols. Of course, that is illegitimate according to most histories of Israelite religion because idolatry comes late in Israel's "religious development."[5] But listen anyway:

> For the customs of the peoples are false;
> a tree from the forest is cut down,
> and worked with an ax by the hands of an artisan;
> people deck it with silver and gold;
> they fasten it with hammer and nails
> so that it cannot move.
> Their idols are like scarecrows in a cucumber field,
> and they cannot speak;
> they have to be carried,
> for they cannot walk.
> Do not be afraid of them,
> for they cannot do evil,
> nor is it in them to do good. . . .
> Everyone is stupid and without knowledge;
> goldsmiths are all put to shame by their idols;
> for their images are false,
> and there is no breath in them.
> They are worthless, a work of delusion;
> at the time of their punishment they shall perish. (Jer. 10:3-5, 14-15)

Then he makes a god and worships it, makes it a carved image and bows down before it. Half of it he burns in the fire; over this half he

5. The important and programmatic exception to that scholarly consensus is the work of Yehezkel Kaufmann, *The Religion of Israel from Its Beginnings to the Babylonian Exile* (Chicago: University of Chicago Press, 1960).

roasts meat, eats it and is satisfied. He also warms himself and says, "Ah, I am warm, I can feel the fire!" The rest of it he makes into a god, his idol, bows down to it and worships it; he prays to it and says, "Save me, for you are my god!" . . . No one considers, nor is there knowledge or discernment to say, "Half of it I burned in the fire; I also baked bread on its coals, I roasted meat and have eaten. Now shall I make the rest of it an abomination? Shall I fall down before a block of wood?" (Isa. 44:15b-17, 19)

Their idols are silver and gold,
the works of human hands.
They have mouths, but do not speak;
eyes, but do not see.
They have ears, but do not hear;
noses, but do not smell.
They have hands, but do not feel;
feet, but do not walk;
they make no sound in their throats.
Those who make them are like them;
so are all who trust in them. (Ps. 115:4-8)

In mocking, doxological fashion, Israel exposes the would-be gods. They are all children of Ludwig Feuerbach, all human figments and projection. The dismissive verdict is not easy in our case, because the Philistines, with Dagon's help, did prevail at Ebenezer and did capture the ark . . . as we have been told five times!

But one must not conclude too soon. One must wait and watch, at least through two nights, when the inscrutable is hiddenly at work. If you watch long enough, the dominant word to be spoken about these would-be divine agents like Dagon who are in fact inanimate objects is "NOT" — *not* speak, *not* see, *not* hear, *not* smell, *not* walk, *not* do evil, *not* do good, *not* save, *not* matter . . . *not, not, not!* Those would-be gods are *not* help but burden. They must be carried. They must be put in place. Their feet must be nailed down so that they are secure in their place. (Obviously the Philistine priests forgot to nail Dagon securely to the floor.) What a sorry, pitiful, empty faith claim! And yet, there are those who prefer the object to the agent, who are always carrying them as trophy, as threat, as "omni," as truth, always nailing them down.

31

But, of course, the negation of the fake gods is not really "background," not really deeply "fraught"; anybody can see that they are inoperative. In the end, Israel is not much preoccupied with the negation of the gods and in fact never utters a word about Dagon. That rhetorical negation is in fact a ploy and a preparation for the real "fraughtness" which is the claim for YHWH, who needs not be carried and who will not be nailed down. Each of these polemics I have cited has alongside the dismissive polemic a doxological affirmation:

It is he who made the earth by his power,
who established the world by his wisdom,
and by his understanding stretched out the heavens.
When he utters his voice, there is a tumult of waters in the heavens,
and he makes the mist rise from the ends of the earth.
he makes lightnings for the rain,
and he brings out the wind from his storehouses. (Jer. 10:12-13)

Thus says the Lord, your Redeemer,
who formed you in the womb:
I am the Lord, who made all things,
who alone stretched out the heavens,
who by myself spread out the earth;
who frustrates the omens of liars,
and makes fools of diviners,
who turns back the wise,
and makes their knowledge foolish . . .
who says to the deep, "Be dry —
I will dry up your rivers";
who says of Cyrus, "He is my shepherd,
and he shall carry out all my purpose";
and who says of Jerusalem, "It shall be rebuilt,"
and of the temple, "Your foundation shall be laid." (Isa. 44:24-28)

Our God is in the heavens;
he does whatever he pleases. . . .
O Israel, trust in the Lord!
He is their help and their shield,
O house of Aaron, trust in the Lord!
He is their help and their shield.

You who fear the lord, trust in the Lord!
He is their help and their shield. (Ps. 115:3, 9-11)

The "fraught" part of the utterance is the assertion that the night transformation is indeed the unseen but decisive work of YHWH. In contrast to the idols who are ciphers, YHWH has real verbs:

> Listen to me, O house of Jacob,
> all the remnant of the house of Israel,
> who have been borne by me from your birth,
> carried from the womb;
> even to your old age I am he,
> even when you turn gray I will carry you.
> I have made, and I will bear;
> I will carry and I will save. (Isa. 46:3-4)

This is a God who carries, makes, bears, saves!

At its most eloquent, Israel stutters to say and name the nighttime work of YHWH. Nobody sees that work. Everyone sees its outcomes; but Israel knows. Israel knows that this God, unlike any other power in heaven or on earth, is indeed a self-starter not moved but moving, not summoned by any other but underway, not authorized by any other but an initiative taker, from ground zero immediately into full speed, from humiliated captive into total newness. The night, it turns out, is filled with the light of life; the silence is filled with the sound of newness; the deepest void is occupied by this relentlessly holy power of YHWH that is not seen but known, trusted, served, honored, praised, and prized. Dagon is a ploy in the narrative. He is there for purposes of contrast, so that YHWH's capacity to devour the powers of death is fully on exhibit. Israel's confessed "fraughtness" concerns the God who bestirs God's own self and all else must yield . . . this God who bestirs in uncalculated fidelity, in unchastened ferocity. This is the one — even the disarmed Philistines and their disarmed god now know —

> who forms light and creates darkness,
> who makes weal and creates woe;
> This the Lord who does all these things. (see Isa. 45:7)

The Philistines, on the third day, are hushed, because now even they know.

33

III

The events of "the third day" create an emergency among the Philistines. Not only did YHWH — in the night, unseen and silent — permanently eliminate Dagon as a rival, but without Dagon the Philistines are defenseless and YHWH is free to act against those who have damaged and humiliated beloved Israel. YHWH's hand, presumably the same strong hand that had toppled Dagon in the night, is now against the Philistines. YHWH's hand is "heavy." The term "heavy," of course, is *kabod,* the same "weightiness" that had departed in chapter 4 on the first day of the crisis. That heavy hand is now back in play. Dagon has robbed YHWH of *kabod,* but only for a moment — well, for three days. YHWH has now recovered YHWH's proper weightiness. YHWH now acts with mean-spirited devastation against the Philistines. YHWH causes, says the NRSV, "tumors." Back in the KJV he used to cause "hemorrhoids." Robert Alter says, in any case, the matter is scatological.[6] We do not know how it is that YHWH can cause such a physical, wide-spread affliction, any more than we know about YHWH's other nighttime work. This agent against the Philistines is the "healer" of Israel who protected beloved Israel from "the diseases of Egypt" (see Exod. 15:26; Deut. 7:15; 28:60). Now this healer is the medical afflicter of the Philistines who brings upon them the "diseases of Egypt."[7] The God who creates "weal" *(shalom)* is the God who can create "woe," the very "woe" of which the Philistines had spoken in anticipation in 1 Sam. 4:7-8. A "daytime" explanation for the "tumors" suggests, perhaps, that the dread and terror produced by YHWH caused bodily dysfunction, perhaps constipation if the affliction is hemorrhoids. In any case, the crisis is the disruption of the natural bodily workings of the Philistines. What the narrator tells us in 5:6 is on the lips of the Philistines in verse 7. The Philistines are made to be grudging, anxious witnesses to the power of YHWH: "His hand is heavy on us and on our god, Dagon."

The epidemic of tumors evokes a civic emergency. The Ashdodites ur-

---

6. Robert Alter, *The David Story: A Translation with Commentary of 1 and 2 Samuel* (New York: Norton, 1999), 27-28.

7. This phrasing calls to my mind the remarkable study of Robert Jay Lifton, *The Nazi Doctors: Medical Killing and the Psychology of Genocide* (New York: Basic Books, 1986). Lifton shows the remarkable and astonishing way in which "medical officers" who ran the death camps could convince themselves that they were "practicing medicine." So much for the "diseases of Egypt."

gently request a meeting of the Philistine Security Council, sensing the great threat to their security. The agenda is "What shall we do with the ark of the God of Israel?" (5:8). What shall we do with this prized trophy that has turned out to be an unbearable threat? In this case, the bad news evidently did not travel fast, for the affliction of Ashdod is apparently not known yet by the people of Gath. The latter are willing and cooperative; they say, "Let the ark be moved on to us" (v. 8). Maybe the Israelite narrator has the Gath city council issue this invitation in order to show how really stupid the Philistines are; they just don't get it! Or perhaps the invitation of Gath is like a rural state being willing to take New York City's garbage for money or their readiness to become a cash-receiving dump for nuclear waste. In any case, the people of Gath foolishly agree to host the devastation.

Within a verse the Devastator devastates the new locale. The rhetoric is intense and sweeping:

> But after they had brought it to Gath, the hand of the Lord was against the city, causing a very great panic; he struck the inhabitants of the city, both young and old, so that tumors broke out on them. (5:9)

YHWH is on the loose among the Philistines! This is a God who "strikes" and produces more tumors. The striking capacity of YHWH is already known among the Philistines, because already in 4:8 they had recognized, "These are the gods who struck the Egyptians with every sort of plague." They know, but they thought they could resist, so that the Egyptian debacle did not need to happen among them. So they said to one another, "Take courage, and be men" (4:9; see Isa. 41:6-7). But within two verses of the move to Gath, the innocent people of Gath are now on notice like the despairing citizens of Ashdod.

This time there is no consultation among the Philistine cities. Things are too freighted with anxiety to take time for consultation. Now there is no invitation from another willing host city, for by now all of the Philistine cities are on notice about YHWH and the ark. The ark is shipped from Gath to Ekron, with neither invitation nor consultation (5:10). The arrival of the ark in this third city evokes a cry, "Why us? Why here . . . ? Why should we be killed by this God, for this is the God who kills and who makes alive, who wounds and who heals" (see Deut. 32:39; 1 Sam. 2:6; Hos.

6:1). The Philistines of course know nothing of life or healing from YHWH. For them it is all wounding and death, death unbearable:

For there was a deathly panic throughout the whole city (5:11).

The hand of YHWH, so the narrative in verse 11 records one more time, was "very heavy" (kovdah me'od). It is all heavy! It is all kabod! It is all about glory! "Ichabod" is banished. The glory has returned, and the news is not good for the Philistines, the great, rejected "other" of the Israelites. Some died. Others did not die but had tumors. Those were the only possibilities offered to the Philistines: option a) death, option b) tumors, no third alternative.

No wonder here was a cry, a loud cry, a cry that went up to the heavens (see Exod. 12:30). Alas, it is a cry not heard in the heavens, for it is a Philistine cry, a cry in cadences not registered among the gods of life. Or at least the narrator cannot imagine a circumstance in which the cry of the wretched Philistines would be heard and heeded as is the cry of Israel regularly heard on high. The narrative has put the term kabod at the beginning as the ark begins to move (5:6), and has answered with kabod at the end in verse 11. The drama is bracketed by kabod. The life-and-death drama takes place in a field of YHWH's recovered splendor of sovereignty. The drama unfolds quickly after the third day, because this raw power over life and death is loosed, and human arrangements to the contrary will not survive its threat and cannot resist its coming.

IV

At the phenomenological level, as Patrick D. Miller, Jr., and J. J. M. Roberts have seen, this narrative is about "the capture and return of divine images."[8] The control of religious symbols, moreover, is immensely important, in that ancient world as in our own. But that is as far as comparative study can go, and of course that is not what this narrative is about, because

---

8. This motif is noted by Patrick D. Miller, Jr., and J. J. M. Roberts, The Hand of the Lord, 1. They note this approach and move well beyond it. See also Thomas W. Mann, Divine Presence and Guidance in Israelite Traditions: The Topology of Exaltation (Baltimore: Johns Hopkins University Press, 1977).

from inside the texture of the narrative there are no comparisons. This account is not about human management or manipulation of religious symbols. This is rather, in a way "fraught" well beyond human management, a testimony to the self-starting of YHWH who breaks the Ashdod captivity. By the flexing of hidden muscles in the midst of the dark, the powerful hands of YHWH begin again. The story is, of course, an Israelite account of the re-gift of life; the Philistines, that "otherness" of death together with their pitiful, phony Dagon, are on notice.

If there are no comparisons, because this God is without comparison and the tales of this God have no counterpart at the level of self-starting action, we turn from comparison to replication and echoes inside Israel, for this God characteristically does what this God does here.

The closest parallel, already on the horizon of Philistine rhetoric, is the Exodus narrative. That narrative, among other signs, is a watchful account of the cry in the historical process. In the Exodus narrative, the cry begins on the lips of Israel:

> The Israelites groaned under their slavery, and cried out. Out of the slavery their cry for help rose up to God. God heard their groaning, and God remembered his covenant with Abraham, Isaac, and Jacob. God looked upon the Israelites, and God took notice of them. (Exod. 2:23-25)

As the narrative moves, as YHWH intervenes in that narrative with plagues that strike Egypt the way the Philistines are struck, the cry disappears from the lips of Israel and moves to settle instead on the lips of mighty Egypt. In Exodus 11, Moses anticipates that transference of pain, because he can attest to YHWH's purpose:

> Every firstborn in the land of Egypt shall die, from the firstborn of Pharaoh who sits on his throne to the firstborn of the female slave who is behind the hand mill, and all the firstborn of the livestock. Then there will be a loud cry throughout the whole land, such as has never been or will ever be again. (Exod. 11:5-6)

The cry will outdo any protest of anguish that Israel had needed to voice at the beginning of the narrative. And of course it happens, just as Moses had anticipated. There is the onslaught of YHWH:

At midnight the Lord struck down all the firstborn in the land of Egypt, from the firstborn of Pharaoh who sat on his throne to the firstborn of the prisoner who was in the dungeon, and all the firstborn of the livestock. (Exod. 12:29)

There is this inevitable moment when power is inverted and the Lord of life and death performs as promised:

Pharaoh arose in the night, he and all his officials and all the Egyptians; and there was a loud cry in Egypt, for there was not a house without someone dead. (Exod. 12:30)

It is precisely this smiting and the subsequent cry that puts Pharaoh, finally, in a mood to release Israel; it has become too costly and risky to retain Israel:

Rise up, go away from my people, both you and the Israelites! Go, worship the Lord, as you said. Take your flocks and your herds, as you said, and be gone (Exod. 12:31-32)

In this text the Israelites do not leave secretly, but are urged to leave as Pharaoh gladly sends them. The same happens in our text, as the Philistines eagerly invite the ark to depart their midst.

The other important observation about the parallel to Exodus is that the turn happens in the night:

At midnight, the Lord struck down all the firstborn in the land of Egypt. (Exod. 12:29)

The turning is more precise than in our narrative, for in Exodus it is at "half night, at midnight." More precisely, but the point is the same: YHWH does YHWH's transformative, hidden, devastating, emancipatory work at night, in the dark, when no one sees and no one can testify. The power for such newness is beyond seeing and the mode of enactment is characteristically obscure. The impact, however, is beyond doubt. In the narrative of the Exodus, Israel is headed to the land, out of the land of bondage. In our text, the ark of YHWH is headed home, out of bondage.

The parallel is evident, except that our text is more radical. Here it is not YHWH's people who are freed. It is YHWH who has freed YHWH's self by a show of devastating power that the Philistines found unbearable. It is power in the night that brings weal and brings woe. The rhetoric is about the "woe" enacted, in sequence, against the Egyptians and against the Philistines. The vantage point, however, is the *shalom* now available for Israel. It is odd how much attention Exodus receives in the tradition of Israel (and in our theological reading of that tradition), while the more spectacular case of the Ark narrative is scarcely noticed. The cases are parallel, except that our case turns from anthropology (human emancipation) or ecclesiology (Israelite emancipation) to theology proper (emancipation of YHWH). The well-being of Israel is a noteworthy by-product of this narrative turn.

But first, it is YHWH's self-emancipation and self-regard that are enacted. This is indeed God for God's self, unable and unwilling to remain in bondage, to be subordinated, confined, restrained, or domesticated. As YHWH later warns David against the confinement of a Jerusalem temple (2 Sam. 7:5-7; see 1 Kgs. 8:27), here is YHWH's ferocious refusal of an Ashdod temple with its implied domestication. Solomon belatedly tried to cage YHWH, to do what the Philistines failed to do (see 1 Kgs. 8:12-30). Solomon's success in that theological effort, however, as Israel learned painfully, is exceedingly provisional.

V

YHWH — the one who is "heavy," whose glory has departed and whose glory is now again visible in the world of the Philistines — is a glory-seeking, glory-getting God. In chapter 4 this glory was gone; now, in chapter 5, the Philistines must reckon yet again with the dangerous, awesome, inexplicable intrusion of that glory into its life and into the life of Dagon. The getting and enacting of glory is quickly and decisively told in this narrative at Ashdod. It is told yet again, later and more familiarly, in the great poetry of exile that seems to derive from our narrative.[9] The 6th-century

---

9. Also to be noted as an exilic articulation of the theme is Exod. 14:4, 17 in the Priestly tradition. On the Ark narrative and an interface to the exile, see Herrman Timm, "Die Ladeerzählung (1. Sam. 4–6; 2. Sam. 6) und das Kerygma des deuteronomistischen Geschichtswerks," *EvT* 26 (1966): 509-26.

exile was a time of YHWH's invisibility, silence, and unresponsiveness. This Isaiah poet among the exiles, however, like the narrator from Ashdod, can sense that the deepest muscles of the Holy One are flexing, that the deepest passions of the "fraught one" are coiling, ready to spring, ready to leap against Dagon, ready to act in Babylon, ready to break the long night of despair and open the day of homecoming.

The poet begins one scenario with a characteristic liturgical invitation:

> Sing to YHWH a new song. (Isa. 42:10)

The old song had died on Israel's lips when YHWH was driven from the field by Babylon, no more doxologies, no more cause to praise. And now doxology is about to be legitimated again. Israel is ready to sing, if only YHWH will provide some ground for the risk of praise. We are told why doxology abruptly becomes appropriate again among the exiles:

> For a long time . . .
>   two nights in Ashdod,
>   forty years by the rivers of Babylon,
>   two more nights by Golgotha. . . .
> For a long time, I have held my peace,
>   I have kept still and restrained myself;
> now, I will cry out like a woman in labor,
>   I will gasp and pant.
>   I will lay waste,
>   I will dry up,
>   I will turn and dry up,
>   I will lead,
>   I will turn.
> These are the things I will do,
> and I will not forsake them. (Isa. 42:14-16)

Summoned to witness and respond, of course, is desolate Israel, long since too weary to notice or to care or to trust. Also summoned, however, are the sea and the coastlands, the deserts and the villages, the entire population:

Let the sea roar and all that fills it,
the coastlands and their inhabitants.
Let the desert and its towns lift up their voice,
the villages that Kedar inhabits;
let the inhabitants of Sela sing for joy,
let them shout from the tops of the mountains.
Let them give glory to YHWH,
and declare his praise. (Isa. 42:10-12)

This YHWH had been eliminated from the screen of historical possibility, eliminated by collusion between imperial insistence and Israel's despair. And now that same YHWH, no longer eliminated, is back in play. The nations will see the "heaviness," the *kabod* — absent, departed, in exile — now present, active, and decisive.

The God who has not mattered for "a long time" now matters decisively and moves dramatically:

The glory goes forth like a soldier,
like a warrior he stirs up his fury;
he cries out, he shouts aloud,
he shows himself mighty against his foes. (Isa. 42:13)

Against the Philistines, against the Babylonians, against all the powers of shut down and death.

For Zion's sake I will not keep silent,
and for Jerusalem's sake I will not rest,
until her vindication shines out like the dawn,
and her salvation like a burning torch.
The nations shall see your vindication,
and all the kings your glory. (Isa. 62:1-2)[10]

The text offers Israel and the nations a great triumphal procession; the very God who had been diminished is now victorious all the way from Ashdod to Gath to Ekron and points north:

10. It is clear that in this text "your glory" is derivative from and reflective of "my glory."

41

In the wilderness prepare the way of the Lord,
make straight in the desert a highway for our God.
Every valley shall be lifted up,
and every mountain and hill be made low;
the uneven ground shall become level,
and the rough places a plain.
Then the glory of the Lord shall be revealed,
and all people shall see it together,
for the mouth of the Lord has spoken. (Isa. 40:3-5)

All flesh shall see. All nations shall notice. All eyes will attend to the *kabod* of YHWH now underway:

See, the Lord God comes with might,
and his arm rules for him;
his reward is with him,
and his recompense before him.
He will feed his flock like a shepherd;
he will gather the lambs in his arms,
and carry them in his bosom,
and gently lead the mother sheep. (Isa. 40:10-11)

No more fear of Dagon. No more submission to Nebo. No more taxes paid to Bel. No more glory ascribed to any of them; they, all of them, are struck, smote, smitten, defeated, discredited, delegitimated:

I am the Lord, that is my name;
my glory I give to no other,
nor my praise to idols. (Isa. 42:8)

For my own sake, for my own sake, I do it,
for why should my name be profaned?
My glory I will not give to another. (Isa. 48:11)

The poet in exile tracks the narrative from Ashdod. The narrative early and the poem late are one in explication of the conviction of Israel that the powers of the night that have stilled and silenced YHWH cannot last into the dawn. For the coming of the light of day turns out to be the coming of the glory of YHWH. The captured, eliminated deity of Israel is on the road again. YHWH's would-be captors in all the cities of Philistia, and in all the precincts of Babylon, and in all the cunning chambers of death that have tried to halt the rule of YHWH all now see, all now cower, all now find themselves in terror; more than that, all now join, relentlessly, awkwardly, resentfully in doxology to YHWH, unable to resist the turn toward home. The very one they had sought to humiliate and domesticate as a trophy has become too problematic and now must be released.

VI

Our narrative in chapter 5 is an account of the way in which the Holy One is seen to be, on the third day, a self-emancipating, initiative-taking, glory-getting God. Our reference to 2 Isaiah, moreover, has shown YHWH to be a God who breaks silence and in a great public, visible way goes home in glory. In the latter text, the exiles go along with the exiled glory and are seen in public with this night-breaking, dawn-rising God (see Isa. 35:9-10; 52:11-12; 55:12-13); the Israelites may accompany, but the imagery is still quite YHWH-centered, concerned primarily for YHWH's own wondrous homecoming in splendor.

The accent on breaking the negating powers — the elemental claim of chapter 5 — is not, however, all focused on YHWH's own future. The same celebration of the return of YHWH's glory also issues an invitation for the transformed life of the people of YHWH. This is evident in the generous imagery of homecoming in 2 Isaiah, though still subsumed under YHWH's own glory. The announcement for Israel is assurance of home-coming:

> Do not fear, for I am with you;
> I will bring your offspring from the east,
> and from the west I will gather you;
> I will say to the north, "Give them up,"
> and to the south, "Do not withhold;
> bring my sons from far away
> and my daughters from the end of the earth —
> everyone who is called by my name . . . (Isa. 43:5-7a)

But then the matter is firmly linked to YHWH's own glory:

whom I created for my glory,
whom I formed and made. (Isa. 43:7b)

In that verse 7, even Israel's well-being is for YHWH's self-enhancement. The matter is transposed in the Psalms, where Israel no longer speaks of YHWH's condition, but focuses upon Israel's own state of affairs. In the temple in Ashdod, all was silent through the night. In Israel, however, the night is not silent or void. There are many groans of death, and every groan is matched by or transposed into a demanding plea to YHWH. The nights when YHWH is held in Dagon's power are the same nights — many nights — when Israel is held bondage in despair. The night is dark and the powers are loose. Israel, moreover, knows that it itself is helpless and cannot compete with the powers, even for its own life. As we all know, moreover, the night can be very long when grief, hurt, sickness, anxiety, despair, isolation, or death are unrelieved. And so Israel, in the long night while Dagon gloats, addresses YHWH:

You keep my eyelids from closing;
I am so troubled that I cannot speak.
I consider the days of old,
and remember the years of long ago.
I commune with my heart in the night;
I meditate and search my spirit:
"Will the Lord spurn forever,
and never again be favorable?
Has his steadfast love ceased forever?
Are his promises at an end for all time?
Has God forgotten to be gracious?
Has he in anger shut up his compassion?" (Ps. 77:4-9)

The night of Dagon's gloating occurs when YHWH's ḥesed, YHWH's "steadfast love," is inactive, held in thrall by the Philistines, when YHWH's promises have failed, when YHWH suffers amnesia and YHWH's anger has vetoed YHWH's compassion. In the night, all the great words of faith tremble and fail; we go over and over them; they are negated by the dark. We are free to believe that the tense, sleepless reckoning of Israel in the night is also what went on in YHWH's own life through those two nights in Ashdod and during the long night of Babylon.

Of course the night with its bottomless darkness may be only metaphor. For the truth is that when one is powerless and hopeless, night may be all the time, night and day; it is all night, even during the day:

> I am weary with my moaning;
> every night I flood my bed with tears;
> I drench my couch with my weeping.
> My eyes waste away because of grief;
> they grow weak because of all my foes. (Ps. 6:6-7)

> My tears have been my food day and night,
> while people say to me continually,
> "Where is your God?" (Ps. 42:3)

Israel knows that "weeping may linger for the night."

But our theme is not the night of dread; we have already done that in our consideration of chapter 4. Our theme is that the night is broken at the dawn:

> When they rose early on the next morning, Dagon had fallen. (1 Sam. 5:4)

> Joy comes in the morning. (Ps. 30:5)

> But on the first day of the week, at early dawn, they came to the tomb, taking the spices that they had prepared. They found the stone rolled away from the tomb, but when they went in, they did not find the body. (Luke 24:1-3)

Chapter 5 stands at the head of a fresh trajectory of testimony in Israel, at the head or as an echo of Exodus dawn, in which YHWH has moved, been aroused, coiled to passion, leapt to newness, all things made new, new enough for a song and a dance and a homecoming:

> You have turned my mourning into dancing;
> you have taken off my sackcloth
> and clothed me with joy,

45

so that my soul may praise you and not be silent.
O Lord my God,
I will give thanks to you forever. (Ps. 30:11-12)

Chapter 5 stands as a great testimony to the self-starting, glory-getting
God who transposes all times, all night to day, all grief to joy, all exile to
homecoming, all despair to newness, all death to life. Now day and night
on the lips of Israel, dawn and dead midnight, are seized from Dagon and
made buoyant:

By day the Lord commands his steadfast love,
and at night his song is with me,
a prayer to the God of my life. (Ps. 42:8)

Yours is the day, yours also the night;
you have established the luminaries and the sun. (Ps. 74:16)

You will not fear the terror of the night,
or the arrow that flies by day,
or the pestilence that stalks in darkness,
or the destruction that wastes at noonday. (Ps. 91:5)

It is good to give thanks to the Lord,
to sing praises to your name, O Most High;
to declare your steadfast love in the morning,
and your faithfulness by night. (Ps. 92:1-2)

If I say, "Surely the darkness shall cover me,
and the light around me become night,"
even the darkness is not dark to you;
the night is as bright as the day,
for darkness is as light to you. (Ps. 139:11-12)

The reason the darkness is now as day is that the light has come. It is the
glory regularly taken to be light. The darkness is dispelled. Dagon cannot
compete in the arena where things are visible. Death has no chance in
broad daylight, which is why Israel is so glad when the dawn comes.

VII

Our theme is the way in which the palpable, strong power of YHWH is able to overwhelm Dagon. Our theme is the capacity of YHWH to break every captivity and end every exile. Our theme is this mighty hand and outstretched arm, the hand that is heavy upon the Philistines, the hand that is severe against Dagon, the hand that is glorious toward homecoming. The rhetoric is primitive, because the life of Israel is bodily and material. Israel has no way to speak of "the turn" in the night except to witness to YHWH's physical engagement with Dagon. That engagement makes Dagon the pitiful loser who now has no hand and no arm, no outstretched arm and no strong hand, no capacity to capture or to exile, no cause to gloat, now fallen and failed.

This narrative is a study in the mobilization of YHWH to create newness. In the Psalms that mobilization is evoked by the petition of Israel, a petition sometimes grounded in pitiful need, sometimes grounded in demanding entitlement as covenant partner, and sometimes grounded in sheer and glad amazement at YHWH. The wonder is that YHWH hears such pleas in the night and acts by sunrise; and to that Israel gladly attests:

> Weeping may linger for the night,
> but joy comes with the morning. (Ps. 30:5)

This is a wonder to which Israel can attest, but can never explain.

The wonder is greater in Ashdod than it is in the Psalms. For here, there is no petition, no covenantal "other" who demands, no partner who addresses, none other who is entitled. There is only YHWH; and yet the passion of YHWH coils, the stomach muscles of the Holy One of Israel flex, and YHWH springs and leaps to newness. No reason for the reversal in the night is given, except the inference that YHWH is not fated, ever, to be an acolyte for Dagon.

In Israel's meditation upon exile, its deep and endless pondering, Israel can indeed voice two grounds for YHWH's self-moving to life. The one ground is *YHWH's faithful attachment* to Israel and YHWH's readiness, characteristically, to intervene for the sake of Israel. This is a grounding in divine love, a grounding voiced deeply by Hosea and Jeremiah, a God moved to pathos by the need and suffering of the covenant partner. It is said succinctly: "God is love." Marvelous and deep as that is, there is no hint of that motivation for YHWH in our narrative. Israel as YHWH's partner is not explicitly present in this chapter, and in chapter 4 Israel is not more than YHWH's fickle partner who must be savaged. At best one can argue that Israel is implicit in chapter 5, because the future of Israel depends upon the curbing of the Philistines and their God. But none of that is explicit here.

The other grounding, mostly neglected in a therapeutic culture, is that YHWH will act *for the sake of YHWH's own reputation.* YHWH will act not out of self-giving love but out of self-regard. That grounding is as old as the prayers of Moses in Exod. 32:11-13 and in Num. 14:13-19 that Katharine Doob Sakenfeld has studied so well.[11] In the Old Testament this alternative motivation comes to its full voice in the tradition of Ezekiel, who has no energy or imagination to speak of God's love for Israel. Rather, hope has to do with YHWH's self-regard, with YHWH's determination not to be second rate, not to be subjugated, trivialized, or humiliated. In this tradition YHWH lives in a shame and honor culture. So Ezekiel 36:

> It is not for your sake, O house of Israel, that I am about to act, but for the sake of my holy name, which you have profaned among the nations to which you came. I will sanctify my great name, which has been profaned among the nations, and which you have profaned among them; and the nations shall know that I am the Lord, says the Lord God, when through you I display my holiness before their eyes. I will take you from the nations, and gather you from all the countries, and bring you into your own land. (Ezek. 36:22-24)

YHWH's reputation has been damaged by Israel the way the sons of Eli had damaged it. YHWH has been trivialized, made light — "YHWH lite" — for "light" *(qll)* is the antithesis of "heavy" *(kabod).* YHWH will reestablish honor and reputation in the eyes of the other gods by restoring Israel. YHWH will do this "through Israel" and "with Israel," but, so YHWH concludes in verse 32:

> It is not for your sake that I will act.

---

11. See Katharine D. Sakenfeld, "The Problem of Divine Forgiveness in Numbers 14," *CBQ* 37 (1975): 317-30.

In our chapter 5 there is no "through you." There is no Israel to save, no Israel that can enhance YHWH. By the time of exile, by the time of Ezekiel, YHWH is now — in the horizon of the other gods — securely linked to Israel and cannot be glorified alone, without reference to Israel. In Ezekiel Israel still does not count in the emotional life of YHWH. It is self-regard that inescapably must be enacted through Israel:

> Therefore thus says the Lord God: Now I will restore the fortunes of Jacob, and have mercy on the whole house of Israel; and I will be jealous for my holy name . . . when I have brought them back from the peoples and gathered them from their enemies' lands, and *through them* have displayed my holiness in the sight of many nations. Then they shall know that I am the Lord their God because I sent them into exile among the nations, and then gathered them into their own land. I will leave none of them behind. (Ezek. 39:25, 27-28)

The action is with and through Israel.

But the ground is more elemental as we push back from Ezekiel to our chapter 5 from which, it seems plausible, Ezekiel took his clue. This awkward, provisional bracketing out of divine love is to push the ground of the break in the night as far back as it can be pushed, to YHWH's own character and to YHWH's own self-regard, to YHWH's own determination to be released. YHWH is resolved to escape Philistine capture, to be in the act of departing and on the way home, and incidentally to leave a few signatory hemorrhoids among the Philistines so that nobody misunderstands what has happened. It is YHWH's determined self-regard that leads to the frantic Philistine conclusion:

> They sent therefore and gathered together all the lords of the Philistines, and said, "Send away the ark of the God of Israel, and let it return to its own place, that it may not kill us and our people." For there was a deathly panic throughout the whole city. The hand of God was very heavy there; those who did not die were stricken with tumors, and the cry of the city went up to heaven. (1 Sam. 5:11-12)

VIII

I have circled this long around these obscure verses of decapitation and disarming — into wider circles of 2 Isaiah, Psalms, and Ezekiel — in order to consider the evangelical question of new possibility.[12] I have used, recurrently, the rhetoric of coiling passion and tensing muscle because I have wanted to reach, as best I am able, to the elemental claim of hope that is nowhere more dramatically and amazingly given in the Old Testament than in the wonder of Ashdod. The tale strikes one as a combination of *a most primitive narrative mode,* an out-of-the-way incident in ancient Israel, and as *large a theological ground for hope* as we are likely to locate in ancient Israel. It is exactly this combination and convergence of primitive incident and large theological vista that is crucial for biblical interpretation.

I raise the question of the church before the text because I believe that given this text, the proper work of the church is testimony against *despair.* I have suggested earlier that the story of YHWH's capture in chapter 4 is Israel's alternative to *denial.* Now in parallel fashion, YHWH's break to freedom is Israel's narrative alternative to *despair.*

It is a commonplace all around, is it not, in church and in society, that much is broken beyond fixing. In the same way, it is clear that so much was broken in the house of Eli that it could not be fixed. In that ancient case, the Holy One declared:

Far be it from me; for those who honor me I will honor, and those who despise me shall be treated with contempt. (2:30)

We would each have our own list of what is broken to contempt, and we would each articulate our list differently. Try this:

• A brokenness of culture, a collapse of the old allegiances that kept life civil and viable, a tumble into mean disrespect, so that the days are filled with fear and the nights with terror;

12. As concerns my own work, I have adumbrated this motif already in "'Impossibility' and Epistemology in the Faith Tradition of Abraham and Sarah (Gen 18)," *ZAW* 94 (1982): 615-34. See the comments of Patrick D. Miller, Jr., *They Cried to the Lord: The Form and Theology of Biblical Prayer* (Minneapolis: Fortress, 1994), 205-23.

- A brokenness of the city, a shrinking of the common good;
- A brokenness of the church, with its layers of alienation that brings to the threshold of schism;
- And beyond all that, where pastors live every day, a disorder, a dismay, a fatigue so deep that it is, for many, beyond managing.

Variously we seek respite in control, which is only an enactment of despair. No newness to be given again, so rearrange the pieces, take control, grab a piece, and secede into a private world. All of that might have been a response of Israel at the end of chapter 4. YHWH had been defeated; the glory had departed. So flee, hide, resist, fend off the Philistines or perhaps join the Philistines, because we are now on our own.[13] Despair is a way of life that stops everything at the closure of chapter 4.

When one breaks *denial* and admits that the ark has been captured, the prospect of *despair* looms, for one now sees how it really is. And now the texted church, the narrators who do not stop at chapter 4, have a crucial word to speak, a story to tell, an imagination to enact, a testimony to render: at the nadir of the night the true character of YHWH acts toward home and will not be held. It is this self-starting God who has always been the ground of hope for the church in its despair. The characteristic liberal antidote to despair has been, against the narrative, the conviction that "God has no hands but ours." The characteristic conservative antidote to despair has been to return to a pre-Ebenezer condition, restore the old priesthood yet again.

This narrative about the self-starting God who breaks the powers of the night, however, does not depend on Israelite hands to defeat Dagon; it has, moreover, no interest in the restoration of what is old and cherished and failed. This God never looks back, but moves in a flamboyant way to newness.

The text, in all its primitiveness, makes a bid for a "second naiveté" that is difficult for those of us so educated and endowed and tenured.[14]

---

13. In the Gospel narrative, the same despair is voiced in these ways:

> Then all the disciples deserted him and fled. (Matt. 26:56)

> But we had hoped that he was the one to redeem Israel. (Luke 24:21)

14. The phrase "Second Naiveté," of course, is the contribution of Paul Ricoeur; but it relates especially to the work of Karl Barth. See Mark I. Wallace, *The Second Naiveté: Barth, Ricoeur, and the New Yale Theology*. Studies in American Biblical Hermeneutics 6 (Macon: Mercer University Press, 1990).

The primitiveness of mode makes it difficult to see how the self-starting God who breaks the powers of the night can break the vicious, sophisticated, and affluent cycles in which we live and create alternatives among us,

- with a culture in demonizing fatigue;
- with a city where poverty of spirit matches material poverty;
- with a church rent asunder in well-intended amendments;
- with that deep hopelessness that besets persons and families who by most criteria should "feel" OK.

Everything failed! Except *the news* that joy comes in the morning. Except *the story* that this unrivaled power for *shalom* will not be held. Except *the conviction* that this God is too dangerous to domesticate.

Notice the categories I have named — news, story, conviction — the stuff in which we evangelicals traffic. These are the claims that seem remote from our failed hegemonic buoyancy, while in lesser parts of the world church these same claims have amazing force.

Wouldn't you like to know in what circumstance this Psalm first got said, or entered the repertoire, or has been used a million times since then and by whom?

Weeping may linger for the night,
but joy comes with the morning. (Ps. 30:5)

It is all a matter of knowing what time it is; and not sleeping late.

(I) *KABOD* HOMEWARD

By the end of 1 Samuel 5 we have observed the regathering of YHWH's glory and the fresh mobilization of YHWH's resolve for sovereignty. YHWH had indeed for a moment at the end of chapter 4 been "glory-less." In that dark moment before the dawn, however, YHWH had coiled and leapt, pushed Dagon off balance, disarmed the Philistine god, and re-established primacy. The Philistines, moreover, had noticed that reassertion of YHWH and had been convinced by the leanly reported data. The Philistines kept noticing through chapter 5 — noticing the terror in Ashdod, noticing tumors in Gath, noticing the cry in Ekron, noticing deathly panic throughout the land — all the notices marked by the narrator in a fresh accumulation of YHWH's *kabod*. The chapter builds until, like the younger son in the parable, the Philistines "come to themselves" (see Luke 15:17) and conclude: "YHWH will arise and go home" (see Luke 15:18). In our narrative, all is now in readiness. At the end of chapter 5, however, we are given only a decision about home, not yet a movement toward home (5:11).

I

The scene, as we move toward chapter 6, is not unlike the organization of a parade at its point of initiation, the marshalling of the bands, the lining up of horses and floats, much discussion, officials with clipboards, walkie-talkies, and frantic gestures . . . pandemonium before the parade begins. When the parade actually starts, everything looks splendid and in order, and the spectators have no clue about the confusion there has been at the outset.

53

The confusion at the outset here features a debate among the Philistine managers of the parade (6:1-10). The civic rulers are all ready to act. They know, however, that the initiation for YHWH's triumphal exit from Philistia must be done with the dignity and finesse appropriate to the winner who exudes glory. For that reason, the civic leaders who intend an evacuation must consult with priests and diviners (6:2). This is a sacred act, a glad acknowledgment of YHWH's holy power that both threatens and heals. The Philistine "holy men" turn out to be good Yahwistic theologians who understand how to treat YHWH with due respect.

The holy men make two responses to the civic leaders. In the first place, they advise that YHWH cannot be sent away empty-handed (6:3). This God has a claim that must be acknowledged visibly and materially. YHWH warrants gestures of obeisance from the Philistines. If a "guilt offering" is presented, moreover, the Philistines can be healed of the tumors that YHWH has dispatched among them. What YHWH has sent YHWH can withdraw from them. The cadences of characteristic Yahwistic conviction reverberate in the ears of the Philistine priests:

I kill and I make alive,
I wound and I heal. (Deut. 32:39)

It is he who has torn, and he will heal us;
he has struck down, and he will bind us up.
After two days he will revive us;
On the third day he will raise us up. (Hos. 6:1-2)

The Philistines can count, and they knew about the "third day" deal. Who knows? The good news of YHWH may extend even to the Philistines — who knows! In the MT, the priests say, "You will be healed and it will be known to you." The versions suggest the alternative given in NRSV:

Then you will be healed and will be ransomed; will not his hand then turn from you?" (1 Sam. 6:3)

The civic rulers ask for more detailed guidance, and the priests respond a second time (6:4-9). They specify that the ark of YHWH must be sent toward home with golden images of five tumors and five mice, gold as something of worth, tumors and mice as tokens of YHWH's massive and decisive action, action that has vindicated YHWH and further debased Dagon and his people. The commodity to be sent along with the ark may be marked by a trace of manipulative magic propelled by continuing fear; it is in any case a deep acknowledgment of YHWH on the part of the Philistine establishment.

The priests, in their utterance to the civic rulers, follow that concrete direction with three theological reflections of a remarkable sort:

- By the gold objects, you "give glory to the God of Israel" with a chance that in response to the gesture YHWH will lighten *(qll)* YHWH's hand against the Philistines (6:5). The juxtaposition of *kabod* ("glory," "heavy") and *qll* ("lighten") is surely intentional. The *kabod* of YHWH has been heavy against the Philistines. If, however, the Philistines willingly give *kabod* to YHWH, YHWH may not need to claim *kabod* so violently, and can ease up on the Philistines. The gold objects as acknowledgment are a salute to YHWH's sovereignty, a readiness to come under that sovereignty that may, in the act of submissiveness, turn out to be more user friendly. At least it is worth a try.

- The priests allude to the Exodus in parallel to the Philistine statement of 4:7-8 (6:6). The Philistines — or the narrator — know that this present Ashdod drama is in the shadow of the Exodus, a replication of that saving miracle. In Egypt, Pharaoh had a hard heart and paid dearly for it. The bid here is that the Philistines should not be as stupid, with hard hearts, as had been Pharaoh. In Egypt Israel stole the silverware (Exod. 11:2). Here the proposal is that YHWH should not be made to steal the gold of the Philistines. Rather, the Philistines should freely and gladly give YHWH the gold. The concession to YHWH is in part cunning, in part prudence, and in part theological awareness that the God of Israel is indeed the God of the Philistines who will be worshipped. The condition of hard-heartedness is most often coupled with the coveting of gold commodities, a nonstarter with YHWH, surely not worth the effort.

- In the end, for all their celebrative affirmation of YHWH, the Philistine priests are not so sure. In something like an anticipation of Gamaliel, the priests end their council by saying (see Acts 5:38-39):

> Watch; if it [the ark] goes up on the way to its own land, to Beth-shemesh, then it is he who has done us this great harm;

but if not, then we shall know that it is not his hand that struck
us; it happened to us by chance. (6:9)

It may be caused by YHWH or it may be an accident. We do not know. We
will find out. But in the meantime, let us be prudent and assume all the
trouble is from YHWH. Act deferentially toward YHWH, even if we are
not sure and not convinced. The entire paragraph is a narrative process
through which the freighted, confused Philistines reluctantly come under
the aegis of YHWH's splendor. They are eager to get the parade under way,
in order to free their land of the threat. They know, moreover, that what
they do in this moment must be done with intentional deference toward
YHWH.

II

Thus the triumphal procession begins, according to priestly specifications
(6:10-12). The ark begins to move; it is loaded with gold. It is pulled by two
milk cows who must decide to desert their suckling calves. The cart moves
and the priests hold their breaths. In the first steps of the cows, perhaps
with some hesitation, it is not yet clear which way it will move. A few more
steps and it becomes clear that the cows are not lingering with their calves;
they have a "higher calling," an act against their mothering instinct. The
ark moves toward Beth-shemesh and the Israelite homeland. The
Philistines heave a deep sigh of relief. The priests now know; the troubles
were not a happenstance occurrence. This is indeed all from YHWH. It is
the same YHWH who now propels the cart. The Philistines are relieved at
the departure. The Philistines are the only witnesses to this beginning, for
in fact there are no Israelite observers (except perhaps the narrator).
YHWH is on YHWH's own with the cows and the ark. The cows are led by
"a higher power," fully obedient to the silent, mute but decisive will of
YHWH to be homeward bound, away from the uncleanness of Philistia,
away from the chipped shambles of Dagon, away from the alien work of
tumors,[1] back to proper habitat with YHWH's own liberated people in liberated Israel.

---

1. I use the term "alien" with deliberate allusion to Isa. 28:21, where reference is made
to harsh judgment. The theme of "alien work" has played an important role in theological
discourse in understanding YHWH's wrath and judgment.

56

It turned out that YHWH did not require Philistine parade managers to get things organized and started. YHWH did not need their permission, nor their mice, nor their tumors. What counts for YHWH is not the Philistine offerings, precious as they must have been, but only the will and resolve to be returning in glory to the proper place of YHWH's glory, among the people of Israel. By default, we may belatedly presume, this glorification of YHWH did indeed "lighten" YHWH's hand on the Philistines. We are not told if the Philistine tumors were healed. All we notice is that the narrator has no more interest in the Philistines or their troubles, no doubt because YHWH has no more interest in them. We are told, a bit later, that the mice and the tumors of gold are on exhibit, presented as a witness beside the great stone in Beth-shemesh, the place where YHWH re-entered Israelite territory (6:17-18). But that notice is likely issued by the tourist office in Beth-shemesh, or perhaps by the Israelite priests who were designated as custodians of the gold. The notice falls outside the dramatic action of the narrative itself, and surely receives no attention from YHWH.

The important point, however, is not the enshrined reminder of the gold in Beth-shemesh that attests to YHWH's homecoming. What counts, what always counts in Israel, is the narrative action. The pivot point is YHWH's self-propelled action in glory, away from bondage, humiliation, and shame, now again buoyant, powerful, and energetic. The power exhibited in this self-propelled triumphal procession in broad daylight is of a piece with the presumed, hidden action in the night when Dagon was toppled. YHWH is irrepressible and is on the way home! Perhaps YHWH en route kept asking the Philistine cows, in eagerness, "Are we almost there?" This is a parade of splendor in which the humiliated God is exalted, in which the captive God is emancipated from all bondage, in which the mocked God is again shown to be unmistakably the God of glory and splendor.

It is no wonder that as the ark approached the fields of Beth-shemesh, the village closest to and most exposed to Philistine encroachment, there was a stir. The Israelite farmers were busy in the field with wheat harvest. But they were not too busy. They looked up and could not believe their eyes. It looked like a golf cart putting along. What they saw looked like a barge filled with nuclear danger sailing along. It looked like something they had never seen before. It was the ark! It was moving at a good pace, led by two Philistine cows who looked determined and were under orders.

57

It took an instant for them to compute what they were witnessing. And then the word trickled down the furrow to the other reapers. The ones resting jumped up in joy; the ones hidden from the heat came to the road. They gathered in exuberance:

> When they looked up and saw the ark, they went with rejoicing to meet it. (6:13)

They understood immediately that YHWH was no longer without glory. They knew for a certainty, but they did not know how, that the power of the Philistines had been broken. Dagon's grip had been overcome. They understood intuitively that the religious turn of affairs implied that the socio-economic, political terrorism of the Philistines was also ended. No wonder they shouted, they danced, and they sang, "free at last," Beth-shemesh liberated!

The welcoming Israelites immediately organized an act of worship (6:14). They split wood, built a fire, and offered a sacrifice. This was not like the earlier Philistine act of guilt offering (v. 3). It was a burnt offering of glad acknowledgment, permeated with thanks, relief, and amazement. The sacrifice is a religious act, but it is at the same time an act arising from the deepest places of economic easement and political emancipation, a religious act that would reverberate back into the public, civic bones of Israel. In this moment of receiving back the self-propelled God again unfettered, the Israelites had an immediate sense that all things were new. It is a moment! It is one of those moments when all in Israel could remember in detail what they were doing in that instant when they saw the ark, or if they were not in Beth-shemesh themselves, in the derivative instant when they heard that the ark had returned, self-propelled, to the borders of Israel, free and unencumbered. And besides that, the ark was loaded with Philistine gold as a submissive gesture from Dagon.

III

The narrative picture given us in chapter 6 concerns the journey of YHWH in glory. YHWH is on the way. In this third lecture, I shall be asking, "On the way where?" As we shall see, the journey of the two cows and the ark is open-ended. The first answer is this: YHWH is, we learn as the narrative moves, *on the way to Jerusalem.* That journey is by stages stretched over a longer period. The ark moves to Beth-shemesh and then to Kiriath-jearim and the house of Abinadab (7:2). There the ark rested, we are told, for 20 years. There is, of course, a long scholarly tradition that the same journey of the ark resumed in 2 Samuel 6, en route to Jerusalem:[2]

> They carried the ark of God on a new cart, and brought it out of the house of Abinadab, which was on the hill. Uzzah and Ahio, the sons of Abinadab, were driving the new cart with the ark of God; and Ahio went in front of the ark. David and all the house of Israel were dancing before the Lord with all their might, with songs and lyres and harps and tambourines and castanets and cymbals. (2 Sam. 6:3-5)

On the older critical judgment of linking 2 Samuel 6 to the earlier Ark narrative, Keriath-jearim is only a way station, for the goal of the ark is Jerusalem. In exuberant majesty, YHWH is headed to the city of David and finally to the temple of Solomon, the ultimate expression of glorious presence in ancient Israel.

The procession in 2 Samuel 6 moves toward David's city; welcome as it is and joyous as Israel is, the ark turns out to be immensely dangerous:

> Uzzah reached out his hand to the ark of God and took hold of it. . . . The anger of the Lord was kindled against Uzzah; and God struck him there because he reached out his hand to the ark; and he died there beside the ark of God. (2 Sam. 6:6-7)

The narrative reports on David's response to that crisis:

> David was angry because the Lord had burst forth with an outburst upon Uzzah. . . . David was afraid of the Lord that day. . . . David was unwilling to take the ark of the Lord into his care in the city of David. (2 Sam. 6:8-10)

---

2. This linkage was proposed in the initial hypothesis of sources by Leonhard Rost, *The Succession to the Throne of David.* But notice the serious dissent of Patrick D. Miller, Jr., and J. J. M. Roberts, *The Hand of the Lord,* who omit 1 Sam. 6 from their presentation of the Ark narrative.

The ark was put into storage for three months, three good months for those who kept the ark.

Finally, in 2 Sam. 6:12-15, David reaches a second judgment, engages in great pageantry, and brings the ark to his newly acquired city, to his recently established tent. David, we are told, shamelessly abandoned himself to the glory, exposing and ceding himself over to the presence:[3]

> David went and brought up the ark of God from the house of Obed-edom to the city of David with rejoicing; and when those who bore the ark of the Lord had gone six paces, he sacrificed an ox and a fatling. David danced before the Lord with all his might; David was girded with a linen ephod. So David and all the house of Israel brought up the ark of the Lord with shouting, and with the sound of the trumpet. . . . They brought in the ark of the Lord, and set it in its place, inside the tent that David had pitched for it; and David offered burnt offerings and offerings of well-being before the Lord. When David had finished offering the burnt offerings and the offerings of well-being, he blessed the people in the name of the Lord of hosts, and distributed food among all the people, the whole multitude of Israel, both men and women, to each a cake of bread, a portion of meat, and a cake of raisins. Then all the people went back to their homes. (2 Sam. 6:12-15, 17-20)[4]

The occasion of David's act is that he received word that Obed-edom, temporary host of the ark for three months, had been blessed by the presence of the ark (2 Sam. 6:12). David, never a man to resist a freely given blessing, promptly engaged the ark. He calculated, on the basis of that report, that the ark evokes an aura of blessing and well-being, even as the ark earlier had been a source of curse among the Philistines, and even to the hurt of Uzzah the Israelite.

There the ark resides with David in a tent. In 2 Samuel 7, David proposes a temple for the ark, but the plan is vetoed "at the highest level." David leaves the ark in the city when he flees from his son Absalom (2 Sam. 15:25), and very soon we are at the threshold of Solomon's new work. Sol-

3. See the full review of the text by Choon-Leong Seow, *Myth, Drama, and the Politics of David's Dance.* HSM 44 (Atlanta: Scholars, 1989).
4. I omit verse 16, as it leads into another narrative issue that does not concern us here.

omon will do what David his father did not and could not do. Solomon houses YHWH's holiness! He builds a temple and, with exotic pageantry of the most extravagant kind, confiscates the ark for reasons of state:

> And all the elders of Israel came, and the priests carried the ark. So they brought up the ark of the Lord, the tent of meeting, and all the holy vessels that were in the tent; the priests and the Levites brought them up. King Solomon and all the congregation of Israel, who had assembled before him, were with him before the ark, sacrificing so many sheep and oxen that they could not be counted or numbered. Then the priests brought the ark of the covenant of the Lord to its place, in the inner sanctuary of the house, in the most holy place, underneath the wings of the cherubim. For the cherubim spread out their wings over the place of the ark, so that the cherubim made a covering above the ark and its poles. (1 Kgs. 8:3-7)

The choirs sang the new theology of presence:

> The Lord has said that he would dwell in thick darkness.
> I have built you an exalted house,
> a place for you to dwell in forever. (1 Kgs. 8:12-13)

The ark is in place, available and settled, permanently attached to Jerusalem and its royal dynasty.

The ark is embedded in and flooded by the glad songs of Israel. YHWH and YHWH's throne now are aligned with the temple and monarchy, and share in the splendor, the majesty, and the dominion of it all. The processional entry all the way from Ekron to Jerusalem (with way stops at the houses of Abinadad and Obed-edom) is perhaps designed for liturgical replication. The liturgy is concerned with assured divine presence, now a guaranteeing presence and not at all threatening. The pageantry of divine entry into the holy place seems clear enough in the liturgical formulation of Ps. 24:7-10:

> Lift up your heads, O gates!
> and be lifted up, O ancient doors!
> that the King of glory may come in.
> Who is the King of glory?

The Lord, strong and mighty,
the Lord, mighty in battle.
Lift up your heads, O gates!
and be lifted up, O ancient doors!
that the king of glory may come in.
Who is this King of glory?
The Lord of hosts,
he is the King of glory.

Some scholars, moreover, believe that the liturgical replication of the processional entry is reflected in Ps. 132:8-10:[5]

Rise up, O Lord, and go to your resting place,
you and the ark of your might.
Let your priests be clothed with righteousness,
and let your faithful shout for joy.
For your servant David's sake,
do not turn away the face of your anointed one.

In that usage, it is clear that the ark is intimately connected to the royal family.

The doors are wide open for the ceremony. The choirs chant and the children watch wide-eyed. In Psalm 24, in four verses, five times "King of glory," five times *melek kabod,* five times "glory" . . . *kabod, kabod, kabod, kabod, kabod . . .* five times king, five times weighty, five times decisive, for "thine is the kingdom and the power and the glory." The paced reiteration of *kabod* surely recalls, for those who know the tradition, the terrible gasp of "Ichabod," the terrorizing power of the hand of *kabod,* and the grudging acknowledgment of YHWH's *kabod* by the hapless Philistines and their hopeless god Dagon.

The marks of this *kabod,* now liturgically contained, are of savage power and terrible abuse, but even more awesome, the capacity to coil and leap, to self-start and to be self-propelled home. And now home here, to Jerusalem, home to David, home to Solomon, home to Israel . . . *kabod . . .*

---

5. Psalm 132 has received full consideration in relation to our theme by Seow, 154-203 and *passim.* See also the classic discussion of Aage Bentzen, "The Cultic Use of the Story of the Ark in Samuel," *JBL* 67 (1948): 37-53.

now quiet, settled, static, and predictable. It is indeed a long way from Ekron and the joy of the peasants at Beth-shemesh to the awesome royal dignity of Jerusalem. It is, however, in the telling all of a piece. The *Subject* of such narrative terror has become, by Solomon's liturgical management, the *Object* of quiet, liturgic adoration.

There are, nonetheless, still memories of the ancient dynamism. Even in this regime at peace under a king named "*Shalom*on," the old wars and old victories of YHWH are still resonant in the Psalm, for this is still

> YHWH, strong and mighty,
> YHWH, mighty in battle. (Ps. 24:8)

At its best, Jerusalem keeps available all of the destabilizing dynamism of YHWH; at its most complacent, Jerusalem stifles the dynamism, for a stifled dynamism is required for the founding and maintenance of a great state and a great corporate economy, the kind over which this *Shalomon* will preside.

In the normative telling of Israel, Jerusalem has always been the goal of the *melek kabod*. Presumably that same dynamism concerning YHWH is not different on the lips of Moses from what we have seen in our Ashdod narrative. Moses sang of the warrior God, celebrated the demise of Pharaoh (a demise of which the Philistines had heard), asserted the incomparability of YHWH, and characterized the dread of Edom and Moab before Israel and — note well — dread of the Philistines (Exod. 15:1-18).[6] The song on the lips of Moses comes, in the end, to

> the place, O Lord, that you made your abode,
> the sanctuary, O Lord, that your hands have established. (Exod. 15:17)

And then the signatory of *kabod* come home, surely to Jerusalem:

> YHWH will reign forever and ever. (Exod. 15:18)

The ark is not specifically on the horizon of this song of Moses. But the cadences are the same. The dynamism of YHWH, by the time of Solomon,

---

6. See the discussion of the Song of Moses by Patrick D. Miller, Jr., *The Divine Warrior in Early Israel*, 113-18.

has come to its proper place of presence and rest. The very term Solomon-*shalom* asserts, "all is well and all is well, and all shall be well."

IV

We have said that YHWH is headed out of Philistine territory *back to Jerusalem,* escorted by the fear-filled Philistines, to make sure the *kabod* leaves their territory. We may ask a second time of YHWH's ark en route home, on the way to where? And our answer is: YHWH is headed out of the Ark narrative *into the books of Samuel and Kings.*[7] The story will not end with the Ark account, but by fits and starts will move to the spectacular character of David, the establishment of earthly power in David's dynasty, the flow of unprecedented wealth and power to David's greater son, Solomon. This family, this dynasty, this city, this establishment, all of whom gather around the ark, bask in the *kabod* of YHWH and count on its promise of power and well-being. The Ark narrative, now in its scriptural locus, has become an episode in the account of the ways in which this indefatigable God moves from strength to strength, until the hidden *kabod* of the night comes to huge visibility in the daytime before the eyes of all the nations.[8]

YHWH clearly has more in mind than simply the ark. Indeed, the narrator has known from the outset where this story is headed. With any kind of theory of inspiration or any conviction about predestination, YHWH has known all of this along with the narrator. It is known in anticipation that the religious drama of YHWH will receive impressive institutional form. We have a clue, even before the Ark narrative, that things are on the move toward monarchy. Already in chapter 2 Mother Hannah serves the larger narrative with the conclusion of her song:

---

7. I have made a distinction between YHWH's venture into the temple city of Jerusalem and into the royal account of the books of Kings, even though the *temple* and *monarchy* traditions are closely intertwined. An argument for a distinction between the two traditions is offered by Ben C. Ollenburger, *Zion, The City of the Great King: A Theological Symbol of the Jerusalem Cult.* JSOTSup 41 (Sheffield: JSOT, 1987).

8. I take the narrative account of 1 Kgs. 10:1-13 as a narrative marker for the way in which the glory of YHWH, mediated through Solomon, is made visible to the nations. That narrative, to be sure, is ironic in its exuberant assessment of Solomon's opulence, an irony made unmistakable in chapters 11 and 12.

The Lord. . . will give strength to his king,
and exalt the power of his anointed. (1 Sam. 2:10)

Hannah uses no proper names. But we know, as does the narrator, that "king . . . anointed" can only refer to David. And of course, it is only a moment after the return of *kabod* in 1 Samuel 6 that Israel argues Samuel and YHWH into a king who can implement the *kabod* in human form (8:4-9). The diversion of Saul is a problem for the narrative, but only briefly.[9] Quite clearly the Saul narrative is used only to point to "the coming one." In chapter 13, with reference to the ill-advised sacrifice by Saul, Saul is rebuked by Samuel:

> You have done foolishly; you have not kept the commandment of the Lord your God, which he commanded you. The Lord would have established your kingdom over Israel forever, but now your kingdom will not continue; the Lord has sought out a man after his own heart; and the Lord has appointed him to be ruler over his people, because you have not kept what the Lord commanded you. (13:13-14)

In parallel fashion, with reference to rescuing Amalek, Saul repents; but it is too late:

> The Lord has torn the kingdom of Israel from you this very day, and has given it to a neighbor of yours, who is better than you. (15:28)

There is a long wait in the narrative from the clue of Hannah in chapter 2 to the promissory pronouncements of chapters 13 and 15. And then, in chapter 16 the future comes to fleshly fruition:

> The Lord said, "Rise and anoint him; for this is the one." Then Samuel took the horn of oil, and anointed him in the presence of his brothers; and the spirit of the Lord came mightily upon David from that day forward. (16:12-13)

---

9. See the assessment of the Saul narrative by David M. Gunn, *The Fate of King Saul: Interpretation of a Biblical Story*. JSOTSup. 14 (Sheffield: JSOT, 1980), an assessment with which I agree.

He was beautiful beyond belief, and the wind came on him. David is clearly the one intended all along, to give YHWH's *kabod* staying power and visible form in the world.

The point, moreover, is affirmed by an odd collection of affirmative voices. Even Saul, desperate, bewildered, failed Saul, is made to know:

> Now I know that you shall surely be king, and that the kingdom of Israel shall be established in your hand. (24:20)

What Saul knows, the prescient Abigail knows in more formal cadences:

> The Lord will certainly make my lord a sure house, because my lord is fighting the battles of the Lord; and evil shall not be found in you so long as you live. (25:28)

And after Abigail, Saul in a reprise is made to confess again, against his own interest:

> Blessed be you, my son David! You will do many things and will succeed in them. (26:25)

In the end, the good word on the lips of the living is yet again voiced by the dead. Conjured from Sheol, Samuel speaks in cranky cadences one more time from the grave. He has changed his mind about nothing since chapter 13:

> The Lord has torn the kingdom out of your hand, and given it to your neighbor, David. Because you did not obey the voice of the Lord, and did not carry out his fierce wrath against Amalek, therefore the Lord has done this thing to you today. (28:17)

The voices turn into a resounding chorus. They are all agreed. The rule of YHWH, so decisive in the night in Ashdod, takes on human, visible form. The oracles so well placed in the narrative of 1 Samuel are now fully enacted in the establishment acts of 2 Samuel. It all happens quickly and tersely:

- David accedes to the throne of Judah:

> Then the people of Judah came, and there they anointed David king over the house of Judah. (2 Sam. 2:4)

The rhetoric toward the people of Jabesh-gilead revolves around loyalty: Jabesh's remembered, erstwhile loyalty to the dead Saul; YHWH's antici- pated loyalty to be shown Jabesh in the future through David and his house. The political turn of power is clearly seen and presented in the con- text of YHWH's abiding fidelity (see 2 Sam. 9:1; 10:1 on the theme).

- David receives, by covenantal assent, the throne of the north:

  All the elders of Israel came to the king at Hebron; and King David made a covenant with them at Hebron before the Lord, and they anointed David king over Israel. (2 Sam. 5:3)

Here the action is even more directly linked to the intention of YHWH, for YHWH has promised the throne to David.

- And of course, after these political agreements and guarantees, David receives the awesome, pivotal guarantee of YHWH through the mouth of Nathan:

  But I will not take my steadfast love from him, as I took it from Saul, whom I put away from before you. Your house and your kingdom shall be made sure forever before me; your throne shall be established forever. (2 Sam. 7:15-16)

David is established forever; already in 2 Samuel 8 we are offered an ac- count of David's remarkable territorial achievements and the amassing of power and wealth. Perhaps David's territorial achievement here is com- mensurate with the territorial achievement of YHWH in the subsequent vision of Ezekiel.

It would have been a very different matter if the books of Samuel had terminated in 1 Sam. 6:1–7:2. But of course they do not and cannot. Per- haps the community of the Ark narrative could have kept the rule of YHWH simple and direct, as Samuel still insists in chapters 7–8. But it could not be. The Ark narrative has been resituated to serve a different ver- sion of the past, a version that governs the sweep of the narrative for which even the God of the ark is recruited and to which that God must sign on. The raw primitiveness of a self-propelled ark now is an item — a powerful symbolic item, but for all of that an item — in the development of im- mense political, economic, institutional power. In chapter 6 this God has territorial ambitions of his own, for the ark crosses the boundary of the

67

Philistines, leaves that territory, and enters the territory which is the normal habitat of this glory, the territory that eventually pivots in Jerusalem. If we peek from the ongoing royal agenda of Samuel-Kings to the priestly vision of Ezekiel, even in Ezekiel 34 where YHWH purposes "direct rule" in light of the failed David family, by Ezek. 34:23-24 even YHWH's direct rule cannot resist one more acknowledgment of the David claim. *The God of the ark* inescapably will become *the God of the monarchy* who pushes the glory to notice among the nations.

This submission of the God of the ark to the glory of David is liturgically enshrined in Psalm 132. The key liturgical claim is that the ark should come to its resting place:

> Rise up, O Lord, and go to your resting place,
> you and the ark of your might.
> Let your priests be clothed with righteousness,
> and let your faithful shout for joy . . .
> For the Lord has chosen Zion;
> he has desired it for his habitation;
> "This is my resting place forever;
> here I will reside, for I have desired it." (Ps. 132:8-9, 13-14)

That movement and settlement of the ark is now deeply Davidic:

> O Lord, remember in David's favor
> all the hardships he endured;
> how he swore to the Lord
> and vowed to the Mighty One of Jacob,
> "I will not enter my house or get into my bed;
> I will not give sleep to my eyes or slumber to my eyelids,
> until I find a place for the Lord,
> a dwelling place for the Mighty One of Jacob." . . .
> For your servant David's sake
> do not turn away the face of your anointed one.
> The Lord swore to David a sure oath
> from which he will not turn back:
> "One of the sons of your body I will set on your throne. . . .
> There I will cause a horn to sprout up for David;
> I have prepared a lamp for my anointed one . . ." (Ps. 132:1-5, 10-11, 17)

The ark's primary business, in this rendering, is the maintenance, sustenance, and prosperity of the Davidic governance.

V

We may ask the same question a third time about YHWH's ark en route: On the way to where? And we may answer: this is the God of Israel departing exile, the way *out of exile to homecoming*. The final form of the text, even the final form of the Ark narrative, has everything transposed by this theme of exile-to-homecoming. Now it is not the Philistines who have detained YHWH, but it is the defining, paradigmatic exile of Babylon. Either way, the land from which YHWH comes is a strange land. Either way, it is a place wherein the Songs of Zion sound strange and the choir chokes in anxiety. Either way it is a place of absence and of yearning, of waiting and of weeping. We should not, in its final form, read the Ark narrative as an old Philistine crisis, because the power of rereading draws everything down into the waters of Babylon or, as we shall see, draws everything through Babylon and out beyond to Calvary and finally to Auschwitz. In the Old Testament, in any case, Babylon is the place where the presence of YHWH is alienated and silent.

The report in 1 Sam. 6:12 is a moment of relief and jubilation when the God of Israel breaks toward home:

> The cows went straight in the direction of Beth-shemesh along one highway, lowing as they went; they turned neither to the right nor to the left, and the lords of the Philistines went after them as far as the border of Beth-shemesh.

The news about the fall of Babylon is a like moment of relief, emancipation, and jubilation. The book of Jeremiah has steadfastly and at great artistic length anticipated the submission of Jerusalem to Babylon. Nebuchadnezzar has been cited as the provisional ally of YHWH (Jer. 25:9; 27:6). But then, as we near the end of the book of Jeremiah, the field is reversed and the news comes that Babylon, erstwhile ally of YHWH, is taken as a defeated adversary. Israel, along with the God of Israel, is free for homecoming:

Declare among the nations and proclaim,
set up a banner and proclaim,
do not conceal it, say:
Babylon is taken,
Bel is put to shame,
Merodach is dismayed.
Her images are put to shame.
her idols are dismayed. (Jer. 50:2)

To say that the city — the city of Babylon — is taken is to echo the news
that Dagon has fallen, beheaded and disarmed. The imperial counterparts
of Dagon are named in the announcement in Jeremiah, Bel and Merodach.
The great displacer, the one who turned the people of Jerusalem into refu-
gees by the canals, has had power broken. The feared city is taken. The de-
spised gods are defeated. The hated images are smashed. These are all syn-
onymous statements in Jeremiah 50.

We have of late watched dreaded, entrenched power fall — in Moscow
and in Johannesburg and in Manila, and in a score of other places, either
already fallen or waiting to fall. It is difficult, in a self-satisfied context such
as ours, to appreciate the depth of exuberance and the adrenalin unleashed
by homecoming. All will be new and all will be new, and all things will be
new.

Ezekiel's remarkable imagination is now to match the dramatic departure of glory in Ezekiel 9 and 10 with the fantastic return of glory in chapters 43–44. As the glory had departed the temple in the face of unbearable
abomination (Ezek. 9–10), so now the purgation of the temple and the defeat of Babylon make possible the dramatic re-entry of YHWH's glory into
Jerusalem. The double context of Ezekiel 9–10, 43–44 is a precise replication of the Ark narrative, perhaps deliberately so. The *departure of glory*
had been due to the priestly abuse of the sons of Eli, so in Ezekiel by
priestly abuse. The *return of glory* had to do with YHWH's powerful resolve to regain dominion. Thus the return is portrayed by Ezekiel:

And there, the glory of the God of Israel was coming from the east;
the sound was like the sound of mighty waters; and the earth shone
with his glory. The vision I saw was like the vision that I had seen
when he came to destroy the city, and like the vision that I had seen
by the river Chebar; and I fell upon my face. As the glory of the

70

Lord entered the temple by the gate facing east, the spirit lifted me up, and brought me into the inner court; and the glory of the Lord filled the temple. (Ezek. 43:2-5)

The sound is like the stirrings of the creator reaching down into the elemental depths of desertion and displacement. The outcome of a "filled" temple intends to parallel and replicate the tabernacle achievement of Moses in Exod. 40:34-38. The palpable *kabod* of YHWH has come back to its proper habitat. A voice speaks from the depth of the glory enunciating YHWH's intention for presence:

Mortal, this is the place of my throne and the place for the soles of my feet, where I will reside among the people of Israel forever. The house of Israel shall no more defile my holy name, neither they nor their kings, by their whoring, and by the corpses of their kings at their death. When they placed their threshold by my threshold and their doorposts beside my doorposts, with only a wall between me and them, they were defiling my holy name by their abominations that they committed; therefore I have consumed them in my anger. Now let them put away their idolatry and the corpses of their kings far from me, and I will reside among them forever. (Ezek. 43:7-9)

At the center of the declaration is the recognition that there has been defilement and abomination, a cheapening and lightening of YHWH's holy name. YHWH has indeed been trivialized, YHWH's "heaviness" mocked. At the beginning and at the end of the declaration, however, in Ezek. 43:7 and 9 there is the parallel phrasing of "forever":

I will reside (*škn*) among the people of Israel forever. . . .
I will reside (*škn*) among them forever.

The formulation is parallel to the song of the choir in the temple dedication of 1 Kgs. 8:12-13. In both cases comes the staggering promise, "forever." Whereas Solomon's choir uses the hard, royal verb "dwell" (*yšb*), Ezekiel more carefully and delicately does not crowd YHWH but employs the verb *škn*, "sojourn, bivouac." No more abuse, no more abandonment, no more absence that permits the powers of chaos to flow freely. The promise is now secure:

This gate shall remain shut; it shall not be opened, and no one shall enter by it; for the Lord, the God of Israel, has entered by it. (Ezek. 44:2)

The gate is shut so none can enter. But the gate is also shut so that there will also be no departure. YHWH will be there, not captured by others, not removing self, not exposed or vulnerable, but now reliable, day and night, for Israel. The departure into exile and the consequent absence had been defining; but it is a one-time event, never again.

In Ezek. 43:12, there is a notation that leads me to a second motif of return and restoration in Ezekiel. In chapter 43, as the glory returns, the plan for a revised temple is laid out; it is asserted in verse 12:

This is the law of the temple: the whole territory on the top of the mountain all around shall be most holy. This is the law of the temple.

The telling phrase is "the whole territory" *(kol gebul)*, all the area within the boundary. The term "territory" is used more than a few times in the final sections of Ezekiel 45–48 concerning the re-entry of YHWH into the land and the re-establishment of dominance and the redistribution of territory among the tribes (see Ezek. 47:15-20).[10] But this usage in 43:12 is of a different sort, because it is of the temple precincts. The same term *gebul* is used only once in the Ark narrative, in 1 Sam. 5:6:

The hand of the Lord was heavy upon the people of Ashdod, and he terrified and struck them with tumors, both in Ashdod and in its *territory.*

I do not suggest that this parallel use is intentional or perhaps even important. The usage in 1 Sam. 5:6 nonetheless is enough to suggest a territorial dimension to the narrative. It is clear that in the triumphal return of YHWH to Beth-shemesh and to Israelite "territory" YHWH is again in the

---

10. See the suggestive discussion of "borders" by John W. Rogerson, "Frontiers and Borders in the Old Testament," in *In Search of True Wisdom: Essays in Old Testament Interpretation in Honour of Ronald E. Clements,* ed. Edward Ball. JSOTSup 300 (Sheffield: Sheffield Academic, 1999), 116-26.

place of YHWH's governance. This is a return to power, authority, and governance, or as we say, "The kingdom, the power, and the glory forever and ever." While YHWH is resituated in YHWH's own proper territory, the narrative accent on the plagues, smitings, and tumors indicates that YHWH has, at least provisionally, established governance over Philistine territory as well, as even the Philistines recognize. The action is a dethroning of Dagon and an enthroning of YHWH, not unlike the dramatic dethroning of Pharaoh in Egypt, so that YHWH becomes the *de facto* and indeed *de jure* ruler of that territory.[11]

The connection between *temple glory* and *territorial control* calls attention to the important study of Ezekiel by Kalinda Rose Stevenson which has as yet not received much critical notice.[12] Stevenson has noted the territorial rhetoric of Ezekiel's vision of restoration and offers the following thesis:

> The Vision of Transformation is territorial rhetoric produced in the context of the Babylonian exile to restructure the society of Israel by asserting *yhwh's* territorial claim as the only King of Israel.[13]

In her careful analysis, Stevenson considers in turn proportionality of the reordered land, control of access concerning who gets into what zones of holiness, and inheritance as entitlement. The outcome of such analysis is the awareness that this anticipated re-entry of glory into residence in Jerusalem is tilted from the religious to the political.

That is, this vision is not simply about presence, but it is about governance. From this Stevenson suggests that the rhetoric of Ezekiel (which may strike one as fanciful and excessively sacerdotal) is in fact a vision of a reconstituted community of power as well as of presence. It is clear, in Ezekiel as in Samuel, that where YHWH re-enters with dominion, power, majesty, and glory, everything must be and will be different. The return is not an incidental matter. Thus to welcome the ark in Beth-shemesh, to receive the ark in Jerusalem, to notice the glory in the temple constitute radical new beginning points of sovereign assertion and wondrous assurance.

11. See Walter Brueggemann, "Pharaoh as Vassal: A Study of a Political Metaphor," *CBQ* 57 (1995): 27-51.

12. Kalinda Rose Stevenson, *The Vision of Transformation: The Territorial Rhetoric of Ezekiel 40–48.* SBLDS 154 (Atlanta: Scholars, 1996).

13. Stevenson, 3.

It is no wonder that the territorial rhetoric of Ezekiel ends, in 48:35, with the announcement:

The name of the city from that time on shall be "The Lord is there."

The return of YHWH from exile, inchoately suggested in 1 Sam. 4:21-22 by the double use of *golah* and the full exposition of the theme in the priestly imagery of Ezekiel, is of course a main theme in 2 Isaiah. At the center of this poetry is the negative declaration that the Babylonian gods will be defeated (Isa. 46) and Babylonian imperial power will be humiliated (Isa. 47). It takes no imagination at all to see in this 6th-century poetic expectation a slow, wondrous replay of the debacle of Dagon at Ashdod. This negative anticipation for the alien deities is matched positively in Isaiah 44–45 by the summoning of Cyrus and his anointing as the current Messiah of YHWH (45:1). The central chapters of 2 Isaiah testify to and expect an inversion of power in the Fertile Crescent wrought by YHWH's own sovereign purpose.

All of that, however, is framed by the vision of a glorious parade, a royal progress of Divine Glory in triumph. The procession is anticipated in Isaiah 35, reckoned with Odil Hannes Steck to be a beginning of the poetry of 2 Isaiah:[14]

> A highway shall be there,
> and it shall be called the Holy Way;
> the unclean shall not travel on it,
> but it shall be for God's people;
> no traveler, not even fools, shall go astray.
> No lion shall be there,
> nor shall any ravenous beast come up on it;
> they shall not be found there,
> but the redeemed shall walk there.
> And the ransomed of the Lord shall return,
> and come to Zion with singing;

---

14. Odil Hannes Steck, *Bereitete Heimkehr: Jesaja 35 als redactionelle Brücke zwischen dem Ersten und dem Zweiten Jesaja.* Stuttgarter Bibelstudien 121 (Stuttgart: Katholisches Bibelwerk, 1985). See more generally Christopher R. Seitz, *Zion's Final Destiny: The Development of the Book of Isaiah: A Reassessment of Isaiah 36–39* (Minneapolis: Fortress, 1991).

everlasting joy shall be upon their heads;
they shall obtain joy and gladness,
and sorrow and sighing shall flee away. (Isa. 35:8-11)

The Holy Way is for God's people. There may be struggles and diversions among God's people, but you cannot miss the road; the highway for the faithful is so obvious. It will be utterly safe and without threat. It will be teeming with God's people coming home, the redeemed, the ransomed, to Zion, singing, joy, joy, joy, no sorrow, no sigh. The parade is here about YHWH's folk, because YHWH does not travel alone. Already in Isa. 35:2 the poet anticipates a glad desert, a celebrative wilderness, the ceding of the claim of every territory to the new governance. . . . Lebanon, Carmel, Sharon . . . all glad to submit to this new regime. The news is good for Israel en route home, but the accent is first of all on the new governance of YHWH:

They shall see the glory of the Lord,
the majesty of our God. (Isa. 35:2b)

The creatures, all of them, will line up on the road to see the *kabod* of YHWH on its way in splendor. There is nothing here about a cart and two milk cows, for matters are now more poetic, lyrical, sophisticated, and elegant. This is nonetheless the same God, the same glory, the same show of power, the same governance, the same joy . . . exile ended, threat vetoed, the end of the nightmare of captivity.

And of course, this initial vision is matched by the better known tour of glory in Isa. 40:3-5:

In the wilderness prepare the way of the Lord,
make straight in the desert a highway for our God.
Every valley shall be lifted up,
and every mountain and hill be made low;
the uneven ground shall become level,
and the rough places a plain.
Then the glory of the Lord shall be revealed,
and all people shall see it together,
for the mouth of the Lord has spoken.

The news is that the powers are defeated and can no longer hold YHWH or the people of YHWH. The poet must press finally to the word "gospel" (NRSV "good tidings") in Isa. 40:9, for the echo of smashing Dagon is a religious claim with huge, newsy socio-political implications. The glory is coming; all flesh observes, all lined up to watch this wondrous, impossible *novum*.

The claim, carried by poetic rhetoric, was not — is never — a point easily embraced in the world touched by the rhetoric. All very well to sing and exude, but the Babylonian gods and Babylonian powers seemed not to yield easily to the force of YHWH. And so the poetry must conclude with a pattern of imperatives and assurances, trying to persuade Israel to take a step home, and by taking a step out of the grip of the empire, to find that the way is open and procession is possible:

> Listen to me, you that pursue righteousness,
> you that seek the Lord. (Isa. 51:1)

> Listen to me, you who know righteousness . . .
> do not fear (Isa. 51:7)

> Rouse yourself, rouse yourself!
> Stand up, O Jerusalem. (Isa. 51:17)

> Awake, awake,
> put on your strength, O Zion!
> Put on your beautiful garments . . .
> Shake yourself from the dust, rise up,
> O captive Jerusalem;
> loose the bonds from your neck,
> O captive daughter Zion! (Isa. 52:1-2)

> Listen! Your sentinels lift up their voices. (Isa. 52:8)

> Depart, depart, go out from there! . . .
> go out from the midst of it . . .
> For you shall not go out in haste,
> and you shall not go in flight;
> for the Lord will go before you,
> and the God of Israel will be your rear guard. (Isa. 52:11-12)

The rhetoric echoes the Exodus of departure. Only this is better than the Exodus — no haste, no unleavened bread eaten too quickly for the yeast to work. You can stay and wait until the bread rises, go at your leisure, at your convenience, but then go. "First class passengers may board at their convenience," utterly safe, protected, surrounded by this awesome bodyguard, not vulnerable . . . but go!

> For you shall go out in joy,
> and be led back in peace;
> the mountains and the hills before you
> shall burst into song,
> and all the trees of the field shall clap their hands.
> Instead of the thorn shall come up the cypress;
> instead of the brier shall come up the myrtle;
> and it shall be to the Lord for a memorial,
> for an everlasting sign that shall not be cut off. (Isa. 55:12-13)

By imperative and assurance the rhetoric that appeals to Israel is of course beyond the Ark narrative, for in that ancient account YHWH moved out alone from Philistine captivity. Here YHWH moves out in grandeur, but does not want to go home alone, wants to carry all the other exiles along with the God of exile. The imperatives suggest resistance on the part of Israel, reluctance to believe that the glory of YHWH is "heavy" enough to outweigh the glory of Babylon (see Isa. 45:9-13). The purpose of the poetry, indeed the purpose of the Ark narrative (and all re-renderings of these texts), is to bring Israel beyond exile — geographical, but also emotional, imaginative, liturgical — confident and trusting enough to take a step beyond empire. This rhetoric is the sort of rhetoric that every venturesome political movement hears from its core zealots addressed to those more fearful and unconvinced. Surely the recent dramas in Prague and Johannesburg and East Timor and the Gaza Strip have been urgings to take a step to find out that the old power of Dagon is a charade not to be feared. It is the imperative of every circumcised community of exiles, every baptized community unsure of its baptism, to share in the parade that appears to be risky but in the end is not, because *the kabod* at the head of the parade is exceedingly heavy.

VI

- The ark has been on its way *to Jerusalem and Solomon's temple.*
- The Ark narrative has been on its way into *the books of Samuel and Kings* and royal, dynastic redefinitions of realty.
- The God of glory has been on the way *home from exile* in Babylon.

Now we may a fourth time ask about the divine *kabod:* on its way where? And we answer: there is another, belated journey of glory to Jerusalem, this time *travelled by Jesus,* the fleshed glory of God. "He set his face steadfastly to Jerusalem" (Luke 9:53). The joyous journey of 1 Samuel 6, self-propelled YHWH, eagerly undertaken by two cows, fearfully permitted by the Philistines, and wondrously welcomed by Israelite peasants in the field, is indeed "a triumphal entry." How could it be understood otherwise?

- A triumphal entry back into the normal territory of *kabod;*
- a triumphal entry *for David,* episode by episode;
- a triumphal entry *from exile,* and all flesh shall see it together.

The only reason the peasants in Beth-shemesh did not gladly shout "Hosanna" is that they apparently did not yet have access to Ps. 118:26. "Hosanna" indeed!

We may look beyond the border at Beth-shemesh to that more familiar entry in Matt. 21:1-11 (see Mark 11:1-10; Luke 19:28-40; John 12:12-19). All four gospels attest to this entry. To be sure, that narrative lacks the two milk cows and substitutes "the donkey and the colt." This time it is Jesus, carrier of the promises of God and the hopes of David, called "Son of David," who comes in royal splendor. As you know, he arrives at the temple, routine habitat of glory; he looks, he cleanses, he claims, he occupies, alarming the squatters who operate the temple and evoking hostility and resistance (Mark 11:11, 15-19). This is his house and his glory comes there.[15]

This Jerusalem pivot, toward which all these several journeys move, is

---

15. On the significance of the temple for the gospel narrative, see Ernst Lohmeyer, *Lord of the Temple: A Study of the Relation Between Cult and Gospel* (Edinburgh: Oliver and Boyd, 1961).

of course the culmination of the sojourn of Jesus as it is the culmination of every journey of the *kabod*. If we may for the moment telescope, it was a freighted week in Jerusalem, just as it was in Ashdod. This journey culminates in Easter, the full articulation of glory, the defeat of all the powers that debilitate and kill, the electrifying event that generates many futures of wonder and transformation and courageous obedience, that endlessly puts every phoney power on notice about new governance over all the territory (see Acts 1:8). Third day indeed!

VII

The triumph of the third day is complete. It embodies a durable, defining assurance to the people of God, an assurance taken to be and found to be utterly reliable, an assurance so sure that it has generated texts reliable and commentary buoyant:

- It is a durable, defining assurance to the vulnerable Israelites who were able to live into a buoyant theology of presence, to gather around the ark *all the way to the temple*.
- It is a durable, defining assurance to the text-makers of *Samuel and Kings*. They never doubted that it is precisely this lord of *kabod* who guarantees the glory of David, and from which they extrapolated the astonishing messianism of David, an opening for decisive human difference in the world, human agency enacting God's own purposes for the world.
- It is a durable, defining assurance to the exposed exiles *who came home* to devise Judaism, the most durable of all committed communities.
- It is a durable, defining assurance for the community that gathers regularly to confess that "*on the third day he arose* again from the dead and ascended into heaven and sitteth on the right hand of God." The one confessed with courage, energy, and imagination is the same one that featured heaviness among the Philistines.

What an incredible assurance! All wrought by the God of tumors who experienced a deep loss of power, but refused to be held by the grip of the Philistines.

Nothing I now say is meant to thin the wonder of that triumphal progress in any way. You will have noticed that in my fourth and last scenario of triumphal entry . . . the one from "Hosanna" to Easter, I skipped over the detail of a Thursday arrest and a Friday death, a Friday death when chaotic things happened:

> At that moment the curtain of the temple was torn in two, from top to bottom. The earth shook, and the rocks were split. The tombs also were opened, and many bodies of the saints who had fallen asleep were raised.(Matt. 27:51-52)

> It was now about noon, and darkness came over the whole land until three in the afternoon, while the sun's light failed; and the curtain of the temple was torn in two.(Luke 23:44-45)

These three hours of darkness are like a long, still night in Ashdod, when the power of YHWH has failed, the rule of YHWH is submitted to others, the glory of God is gone into its exile.

Friday is more than a blip in the flow from Sunday to Sunday. It is a staggering, deconstructive description on which our faith pivots. It becomes a warrant for noticing the deconstructive interruption in each of these journeys of *kabod*, for Israelite narrators and singers knew that the momentary capture of glory leaves an abiding tattoo on the God of glory. The assurance of triumph is tempered by a notice, and a wait, and endless dark nights. The assurances are matched by an abiding candor about this God of whose ark it must be said five times, "It was captured." Nothing that happens in 1 Samuel 5–6 can undo or obliterate the stark truth of chapter 4:

- YHWH in glory had gone up to Jerusalem, the ark finally coming to rest in Solomon's temple midst exotic pageantry. But a *deconstructive note is added by a custodian* in the temple, for custodians tend to see through the pageantry and tell the less dramatic truth of the matter:

> There was nothing in the ark except the two tablets of stone that Moses had placed there at Horeb, where the Lord made a covenant with the Israelites, when they came out of the land of Egypt. (1 Kgs. 8:9)

The ark is empty! Perhaps the custodian did not have eyes to see. Or perhaps the *kabod*, as restless as the janitor is honest, departed the overheated temple pageant for an instant. In any case, what is there is only "the tablets of stone," only Torah, only obedience, not glory. This minimalist trace permits the narrator to add, in 1 Kgs. 9 just after the hullabaloo of chapter 8, a stern "if-then" of Torah (1 Kgs. 9:4-9). That addendum indicates that the glory is surrounded by the demands of Torah, for this glory is about an alternative community of obedience and not just a religious glow.

- YHWH in glory had gone on into 1 and 2 Samuel, finally arriving at the guaranteed splendor of David. The literature is royal, all about kings, all about this family as the permanent carrier of God's sovereign intention. But of course, the great oracle of guarantee in 2 Samuel 7 is only a few pages before the narrative of shabbiness and cynicism with Uriah and Bathsheba (2 Sam. 11:1-27), the oracle of Nathan (2 Sam. 12:7-12), and then the oracle of Ahijah against David's greater son (1 Kgs. 11:31-39), narrative and oracle about ending, termination, and shame, disgrace, and loss. Time would fail me to tell of David's later sons, of Ahaz, of Manasseh, of Jehoiachim, of loss, of failure, of judgment, of deportation. Until finally the royal claimants must ask:

Lord, where is your steadfast love of old,
which by your faithfulness you swore to David? (Ps. 89:49)

- YHWH in glory had gone up out of Babylon, just as Ezekiel had envisioned and as 2 Isaiah had dramatized. It was a re-entry of joy and shalom, and all flesh could see it happening. Except that immediately the disputes had to be undertaken, and the disputatious, quarrelsome destiny of Judaism derived from the vision. Immediately came the Ezekiel question concerning which priests had authority to do what (Ezek. 44:9-17).[16] The Isaiah community, moreover, disputed immediately about who was to get in and who was kept out, a question of ethnic exclusion and exclusion by sexual condition (Isa. 56:3-8). Belatedly,

---

16. On the dispute among priestly orders concerning the control of the temple, see the somewhat overly schematic analysis of Paul D. Hanson, *The Dawn of Apocalyptic: The Historical and Sociological Roots of Jewish Apocalyptic Eschatology*, rev. ed. (Philadelphia: Fortress, 1979).

81

Haggai still has his eye on YHWH's *kabod*. And so he speaks of the destroyed temple:

Who is left among you that saw this house in its former *glory?* (Hag. 2:3)

It was glory that was and now is gone, a temple celebrated by Solomon but not sustained. To be sure, the oracle of YHWH anticipates a new house of glory:

Go up to the hills and bring wood and build the house, so that I may take pleasure in it and be *honored,* says the Lord. (Hag. 1:8)

But not now, not yet, not in hand. It is for good reason that Zechariah terms the day a day of "littleness" (Zech. 4:10), a day of diminishment, little glory of YHWH, less for Israel, much less than the glory anticipated by either Ezekiel or 2 Isaiah.

- YHWH in glory is embodied in Jesus, but it is a crucified glory, a Friday glory that even on Sunday comes out marked by woundedness, a different sort of glory. Paul says:

None of the rulers of this age understood this; for if they had, they would not have crucified the Lord of glory. (1 Cor. 2:8)

The text is left always with a decisive interruption of deconstruction, a Lord of glory with a residue of absence and pain.

It would not have been said this way in the Ark narrative per se; but even taken per se, the Ark narrative ends with a great slaughter of God's own people, a harsh glory in which Israelites fare no better than the Philistines:

The descendants of Jeconiah did not rejoice with the people of Beth-shemesh when they greeted the ark of the Lord; and he killed seventy men of them. (1 Sam. 6:19)[17]

17. Notice should be taken of the seemingly parallel narrative note in 2 Sam. 6:6-7 concerning Uzzah. On the latter, see the ritual interpretation of Seow, *Myth, Drama,* 97-104. On

But we do not have an Ark narrative. We have an Ark narrative resituated and reread about the coming and going of glory, but not yet a final coming. The ark is headed for Jerusalem. Jerusalem is the pivot point and center of its story. Israel celebrates, but Israel also knows that for all the wonder of *kabod*, Jerusalem is a complex pivot, a promised residence for glory, a failed residence for glory, an inadequate and finally "empty" residence for glory, yet again promised.

VIII

Now, I have spent long on the *assurances* intrinsic to the Ark narrative and then less time on *assurances deconstructed*. In its sober reuse, the Ark narrative, so filled with assurance, tells powerfully against any assurance too closely held. That is, the triumph of YHWH tells against every triumphalism. I tilt my interpretation in this direction precisely because triumphalism is a deep threat to the triumph of Easter faith.

The temptation of triumphalism is an old one in our theological tradition, as old as "no salvation outside the church," a temptation now echoed in the shameless claim of liberals and conservatives to know fully the mind of Christ on all the issues of the day, a claim not yet congruent with the place of pluralism where God has put us.

As the *assurance* tells against every loss of nerve, so the *break* tilts against every excessive buoyancy in the name of faith. Carl Becker has shown how readily, in the 18th century, the theological citadel of glory was transposed into the controlling power of reason.[18] I suggest that this same "theology of glory" that issues in decisive triumph is now carrying us into a U.S.-dominated globalism that feels like the triumph of our election as God's people. Francis Fukuyama, of course, has stated the claim most dramatically, but, with the vitality of consumer capitalism helped along the way by reshaping technology, our present is surely a win for the "good guys."[19] To preside over this remarkable generativity of wealth, power, and control is not unlike,

---

the relationship of the two episodes, see P. Kyle McCarter, Jr., *II Samuel.* AB 9 (Garden City: Doubleday, 1984), 169-70.

18. Carl Lotus Becker, *The Heavenly City of the Eighteenth Century Philosophers* (New Haven: Yale University Press, 1932).

19. Francis Fukuyama, *The End of History and the Last Man.*

the welcome to Beth-shemesh,
or the temple dedication,
or the dynastic oracle,
or the procession from Babylon.

The narrative reread permits us to see that the glory is wounded, exile-sobered, Friday-scarred, and Auschwitz-candid. The very glory Israel had in hand turned out to be threat. And beyond threat, a long waiting. It does not surprise us, with the buoyancy of glory now fully visible and seemingly in hand, that the people of Beth-shemesh, echoing the Philistines, had to ask in fear and trembling perplexity:

To whom shall he go so that we may be rid of him? (1 Sam. 6:20)

In their dread they pondered:

Who is able to stand before the Lord, this holy God? (6:20)

And we who come later ponder the wound, the scar, the sobering, the candor, and echo, "Who indeed?"

THE BIBLE STRANGE AND NEW

When I discussed these Stone lectures with Bernhard Anderson, that greatly beloved Princeton man, he said to me, "For the Stone Lectures you will want a very large theme." Now you may think that thus far into these lectures, I have had a rather small theme, nothing more than the Ark narrative, a brief, canonically bracketed, seemingly primitive, likely old narrative that is promptly overcome in the final form of the text by the rise of David. Perhaps you have also noticed, however, that my concern has not been primarily with the Ark narrative, but with what Professor Anderson would agree is "a very large theme," namely, what is it that the church does when it stands before the biblical text? I have taken up the Ark narrative as a way into that large and important question, because I believe that abstract and speculative answers to the question of the use of Scripture are of no help at all; our answer must be in quite specific textual practice.

I

There is no doubt that the question — what does the church do when it stands before the text — has recurring and perennial answers that consistently arise in the long history of the church. It is equally clear, however, that the particular answer to that question is quite context specific, and in each new time, place, and circumstance, the church must work out afresh what it means to stand before the text; thus in every time and place the answer that the church gives is in part a long tested one in the church and in part our own fresh take, for which we are immediately responsible.

85

Concerning our answer to the question now in the U.S. church where our conventional claims in the Reformed tradition are radically deprivileged, my attempt is to insist that our listening to, hearing, reading, interpreting, and obeying the biblical text must be as deeply *nonfoundational* as possible;[1] that is, our posture before the text requires not reading according to the assumptions — theological, historical, or cultural — that are so authoritative all around us. The reason for such a stand is that, so it seems to me, the consciousness and discourse of the church in both its liberal and its conservative manifestations are to some great extent contained in modes and assumptions about knowledge that are modernist and postmodernist in ways that I would characterize as "technological-consumerist."

I do not want here to tarry in all the analyses that are appropriate to issues of "modernism" and "postmodernism"; it is clear in any case that both the radically autonomous reason of modernism and the out-of-control subjectivism of much postmodernism pertain in equal measure.[2] For our purposes the phrasing of "technological consumerism" refers not only to the depersonalizing of computerism but to the awareness that all of the new technologies serve first of all our U.S. military monopoly in the world, and our technological consumerism bespeaks a self-indulgent commoditization whereby the human fabric of our common life is alarmingly diminished. Perhaps the most flamboyant celebration of this mode of life is found in the relatively uncritical articulations of Francis Fukuyama, but I believe that in less celebrative, less obvious, and less buoyant forms the claims of this way of life are powerfully pervasive and persuasive among us.[3] I have, moreover, no case to make that such a perspective is more a conservative or more a liberal temptation, for I believe it to be a powerful

1. For an accessible review of the issues, see John E. Thiel, *Non-foundationalism* (Minneapolis: Fortress, 1994). See the recent suggestive piece by Francis Schussler Fiorenza, "Fundamental Theology and Its Principle Concerns Today: Towards a Non-Foundational Foundational Theology," *Irish Theological Quarterly* 62 (1996/97): 118-39; and more broadly, Stanley J. Grenz and John R. Franke, *Beyond Foundationalism: Shaping Theology in a Postmodern Context* (Louisville: Westminster John Knox, 2001); and F. LeRon Shults, *The Postfoundationalist Task of Theology: Wolfhart Pannenberg and the New Theological Rationality* (Grand Rapids: Wm. B. Eerdmans, 1999).

2. See my own discussion of these issues in *Texts Under Negotiation: The Bible and Postmodern Imagination* (Minneapolis: Fortress, 1993).

3. Francis Fukuyama, *The End of History and the Last Man.*

option across the spectrum of opinion, for the filter of reading the Christian tradition, for the hearing of the gospel, and, insofar as we are an assemblage of preachers, for the speaking of the gospel. Nor do I believe, as concerns our disputatious modernist, postmodernist environment, that it is so dark that all cats are gray and distinctions cannot be made. Indeed, distinctions can and must be made. But that issue for the moment does not concern me here.

Rather, if my characterization of our environment for contemporary Christian preaching, worship, faith, and life is roughly correct — and I do not see that it can be doubted — then the question is how far and in what ways can the biblical text be heard among us as an authoritative voice that is a genuine alternative that is not from the outset turned and trimmed by the pressures, demands, and attractions of the dominant account of reality that is everywhere among us. I freely acknowledge, moreover, that every attempt to read and hear outside that dominant pressure is at best a partial, compromised one, for we who seek to do so are ourselves no doubt "kept" women and men who do not want and are not able to go very far. With all of that qualification, however, my probe and wonderment are to see how far and in what ways "text time" in the church is a time of genuine alternative that cuts deeply into our identity and that reaches broadly into our daily life.

In my discussion of that question, I will try to track some unfinished business from my *Theology of the Old Testament* from 1997 in a way that I intend to be useful and not defensive.[4] There I have staked out a nonfoundational position that does not owe too much to the highly visible nonfoundationalism of Stanley Hauerwas, both because I have proceeded in a Reformed fashion as he does not, and because I am an exegete and reader of texts in a way that he is not and does not intend to be.[5] This occasion provides for me a chance to clarify and give nuance to what I have said there. In terms of the interpretive options that are before us, I propose that a nonfoundational approach, an attempt to give voice to a deep alternative

4. Walter Brueggemann, *Theology of the Old Testament: Testimony, Dispute, Advocacy* (Minneapolis: Fortress, 1997).

5. See especially Stanley Hauerwas and William H. Willimon, *Resident Aliens: Life in the Christian Colony* (Nashville: Abingdon, 1989). A Reformed accent is represented, for example, by Douglas John Hall, *Confessing the Faith: Christian Theology in a North American Context* (Minneapolis: Fortress, 1996), 255, with his aphorism, "Disengage in order to re-engage"; see 251, 325, 332, and *passim*.

that is given in the text and that is not particularly respectful of our preferred inclinations and modes of reasoning, liberal or conservative, is
worth our attention and effort.

1. That deep alternative suggests to me that we must not pay too
much or primary attention to questions of "history," that is, must not ask
too soon "what happened?"[6] For that question is almost always promptly
transposed into the skeptical wonderment, "Could that have happened?"
The two questions — what happened, what could have happened — trim
the textual claim very soon to make it conform to the acceptable "historical" horizons of the day.[7] Indeed, one can claim that the entire critical
project, right up until the Jesus Seminar, is to give veto power to whatever
contours of "happenedness" are currently fashionable. It is clear that the
text and its primal listening community were not governed too soon by
that question which surfaces quickly in our modern-postmodern consciousness.

2. That deep alternative suggests to me that we must not pay too much
or primary attention to the "dominant rationality" of our time and place,
in our case the assumptions and allowances of Enlightenment modernity.
This is in fact the "question of history" writ large, for Enlightenment rationality from the outset has taken aim at the "wonders" claimed in the biblical text, and by the vagaries of "historical criticism" has explained them
away, emptying the text, where it can, of its alternative voice.[8]

3. That deep alternative suggests to me that we must not pay too much
or primary attention to the settled theological claims of the Christian tradition, for those settled claims have always tended to move toward a coherence that, wittingly or not, has worked to mute the shrillness and
disjunctions that are crucial to the disclosing process of the text itself.[9] The
settled theological tradition, moreover, has always been at first formula-

6. See Brueggemann, *Theology of the Old Testament*, 118.
7. See the shrewd refinement of the issue by Norman K. Gottwald, "Rhetorical, Historical, and Ontological Counterpoints in Doing Old Testament Theology," in *God in the Fray: A
Tribute to Walter Brueggemann*, ed. Tod Linafelt and Timothy K. Beal (Minneapolis: Fortress, 1998), 11-23.
8. See Rebecca S. Chopp, "Theology and the Poetics of Testimony" (unpublished
manuscript), on the disjunction of "theory" and "testimony," and more specifically her
comment on Lessing, who makes "reason" the judge and orderer of "history."
9. See Chopp, on the power of testimony to create disjunction in every theoretical
claim for truth.

tion profoundly contextual but then subsequently absolutized, whether contextual to the great philosophic formulations of the 3rd and 4th and then 13th centuries, or to the scientific requirements of the 17th century, eventually creating coherences that have readily overridden the detailed clues, traces, and problematics of the text itself, wherein may lie much of the transformative power of the text.[10]

I understand, as my critics have made abundantly clear to me, that such a provisional and cautionary resistance to the defining power of *history, reasonableness,* or *doctrinal consensus* is a high-risk undertaking, and perhaps I have not articulated my intention very well. I have intended, in 1997 and now, that these considerations of history, reasonableness, and doctrinal consensus be provisionally bracketed out as a strategic maneuver, and not as a nullification; for I have no doubt that eventually we do learn a great deal from history, reasonableness, and the doctrinal consensus tradition that concerns the text. But I suggest that this occur not first, not soon, not too quickly, in order that the surprise, gift, and threat of a genuine alternative in the text should not be excluded in principle from our hearing before we have even listened.

In these lectures I have thus far tried to listen to the text of the Ark narrative without raising too soon any of the disciplining questions of history, reasonableness, or doctrinal consensus, in order to see if a kind of innocence, albeit a "second naiveté," might yield a fresh reading.[11] It is my thought that at the turn of the millennium, as we live, work, interpret, and believe in a society that is coming unglued, that the church stands before the text to listen for a disclosure that is a genuine alternative to the defining power of technological consumerism, precisely because it is only in that genuine alternative that energy, power, and authority for missional initiative will be given. I submit that much of the feebleness and frustration of the church in its present state is because it is not a welcome habitat for a genuine alternative; in our Reformed tradition, it is this text to which we finally turn. That is my theme for which the Ark narrative may be a test case, one I hope Professor Anderson will think is large enough.

---

10. See the comments of Joseph Dan, "Midrash and the Dawn of Kabbalah," in *Midrash and Literature,* ed. Geoffrey H. Hartman and Sanford Budick (New Haven: Yale University Press, 1986), 127-31.

11. See Mark I. Wallace, *The Second Naiveté: Barth, Ricoeur, and the New Yale Theology.*

II

In my essay on the authority of Scripture in *The Anchor Bible Dictionary,* I appealed to both Karl Barth and Martin Buber for the most poignant essays on the issue of authority.[12] These two awesome figures, I suggested, may be usefully twinned as Jew and Christian concerning the peculiar authority of Scripture. And now, as I had not seen then, I take Barth and Buber to offer twinned statements of radical nonfoundationalism, though the phrase was not on the horizon in their time of writing.

Karl Barth with his commentary on Romans in 1919 needs no mention in this company, and no additional appreciation for its extraordinary and enduring power among us. In our context, however, it is worth noticing that Barth faced the problem that the Bible, of course including the letter to the Romans, had in his context been completely submerged in the dominant "liberal" ideology so that the Bible had not enough power to be heard as a genuine alternative. His great insight (first I wrote "incite") and electrifying summons was the assertion that the biblical text was indeed a deep alternative to the dominant ideology of his day. His proposal was indeed nonfoundational, for he wanted to find a place outside the dominant account of reality that had so mesmerized the church as it had falsely assured the surrounding culture. It cannot be unimportant, of course, that he was, in his nonfoundationalism, a pastor. It may be wondered (at least by me), as he became an academic, whether he became increasingly foundationalist as academics are wont to do. That, however, is not now our question. Our interest is that at the outset he was readily nonfoundationalist in hearing the text as alternative, and it is in its alternativeness that the Bible tells the news of a different future offered by the Gospel to the world.

Behind the *Römerbrief,* among other things, is his well-known church address from 1916, "The Strange New World within the Bible," in which Barth is at his most nonfoundationalist.[13] Barth begins with his repeated question, "What is there within the Bible?"[14] As you know, he proposes three conventional answers to his question, only to reject them:

12. Walter Brueggemann, "Biblical Authority in the Post-Critical Period," *ABD* 5:1049-56.

13. Karl Barth, "The Strange New World Within the Bible," *The Word of God and the Word of Man* (New York: Harper & Row, 1957), 28-50.

14. Barth, 28.

- His first answer is that there is *history* in the Bible . . . but Barth quickly judges that what is going on here is hardly history with its series of causes and consequences, for a concern for "history" is a long leap from the sovereign hiddenness and intrusiveness of God. Barth concludes:

> When God enters, history for the while ceases to be, and there is nothing more to ask; for something wholly different and new begins — a history with its own distinct grounds, possibilities, and hypotheses. . . . A new world projects itself into our old ordinary world. We may reject it. We may say, It is nothing; this is imagination, madness, this "God." But we may not deny nor prevent our being led by Bible "history" far out beyond what is elsewhere called history — into a new world, into the world of God.[15]

- Barth's second candidate for what is in the Bible is *morality;* but of course that yields nothing either in Barth's purview.[16]
- And then, third, *religion,* which of course never gets Barth anywhere.[17]

With all of these options closed what is there is God, word of God, God's world:

> We have found in the Bible a new world, God, God's sovereignty, God's glory, God's incomprehensible love. . . . What is the mysterious "other," new, greater world which emerges in the Bible beyond all the ways of men, summoning us to a decision to believe or not to believe? . . . He purposes naught but the establishment of a new *world* . . . The Holy Spirit establishes the righteousness of heaven in the midst of the unrighteousness of earth and will not stop nor stay until all that is dead has been brought to life and a new *world* has come into being.[18]

The last two times quoted, the term "world" is in italics in the English text. Now of course, in this surge of newness Barth did not speak with any care-

15. Barth, 37.
16. Barth, 37.
17. Barth, 41.
18. Barth, 45, 49, 50.

ful precision with the term "world." Nevertheless, his rhetoric does sound like that of Paul Ricoeur's later "world in the text and world in front of the text," precisely refusing any appeal to the old "world behind the text."[19] It is clear that world uttered by the Bible cannot have its foundation in that world "behind the text" where historians tend to ply their trade. This world of God found in the Bible is more than an existential meeting with God; it is a *world,* a network of relationships, an account of all the spheres of power and money now regrounded and reissued in the news of the God of heaven even on earth. This is what Barth found in the Bible in his stubborn refusal of foundationalism, without appeal to any prejudgment of history, morality, or religion.

III

Martin Buber's complementary essay was a lecture in 1926, republished in English in 1948, entitled "The Man of Today and the Jewish Bible."[20] Buber speaks of "the man of today" who cannot make contact with the Bible, the man of industry captured by Cartesian autonomy that has issued in technological consumerism. Of this man, Buber writes:

> He must read the Jewish Bible as though it were something entirely unfamiliar, as though it had not been set before him ready-made, as though he has not been confronted all his life with sham concepts and sham statements that cited the Bible as their authority. He must face the Book with a new attitude as something new. He must yield to it, withhold nothing of his being, and let whatever will occur between himself and it. . . . He holds himself open. He does not believe anything a priori; he does not disbelieve anything a priori. He reads aloud the words written in the book in front of him; he hears the word he utters and it reaches him. Nothing is prejudged. . . . In order to understand the situation fully, we must

19. Ricoeur has discussed this in many places. Among his earliest references in "The Hermeneutical Function of Distanciation," *Hermeneutics and the Human Sciences — Essays on Language, Action and Interpretation* (Cambridge: Cambridge University Press, 1981), 131-44, esp. 143. I am grateful to my colleague George Stroup for this particular reference.

20. Martin Buber, "The Man of Today and the Jewish Bible," *On the Bible: Eighteen Studies* (New York: Schocken, 1968), 1-13.

picture to ourselves the complete chasm between the Scriptures and the man of today.[21]

The man of today, so Buber, has real problems:

> The man of today knows of no beginning. As far as he is concerned, a history ripples toward him from some prehistorical cosmic age. He knows of no end; history sweeps him on into a posthistorical cosmic age. What a violent and foolish episode this time between the prehistorical and the posthistorical has become! Man no longer recognizes an origin or a goal because he no longer wants to recognize the midpoint. . . . Man of today resists the Scriptures because he cannot endure revelation. . . . Man of today resists the Scriptures because he no longer wants to accept responsibility. He thinks he is venturing a great deal, yet he industriously evades the one real venture, that of responsibility.[22]

Following Franz Rosenzweig, Buber asserts that *revelation* is the midpoint of *creation* and *consummation,* and that it is the "strangeness" of biblical concepts that constitutes "the stone of stumbling."[23] Buber's urging then is that the man of today finds himself addressed by a voice that is strange:

> He listens to that which the voice, sounding forth from this event [Sinai], wishes to communicate to him its witness, to his constitution, to his life, to his sense of duty. It is only when this is true that man of today can find the approach to biblical reality.[24]

To be sure, there are important differences between Barth and Buber, not only the inescapable difference of Jew and Christian, the difference between Sinai and Christ. Buber is much more inclined to credit the psychology of human receptivity, while Barth of course comes to claims completely from the other side. Having said that, however, the two speak with a single voice. Their cadences are remarkably similar concerning strange-

21. Buber, 5.
22. Buber, 7.
23. Buber, 8.
24. Buber, 9.

ness, revelation, newness, and a gift from beyond us. Barth in the midst of World War I (1916), Buber during the Weimar Republic (1926), both reflect on the power of modernity to deceive. Odd, is it not, that the Jewish Buber had to face the same reality as did the Christian Barth; they faced the condition of the Western world when the Bible was seen as a reference point outside the deep failure of the Western ideology of control. They concluded the Bible to be strange, a dramatic way of asserting nonfoundationalism beyond all comfortable presuppositions of history, reason, or doctrine. Their time required such a strangeness; it is to their awesome credit that they saw fully the strangeness.

Now, I linger this long over Barth and Buber not only because of their astonishing assertions on the Bible, and not only because they are nonfoundational, appealing to the Bible in the raw. I linger because I wonder if at the end of the 20th century and the turn of the millennium we are not in a context ripe for radical news of a strange textual kind as was the West after the failure of 19th-century optimism, World War I, Versailles, and National Socialism soon to come in its barbarism. Theirs was a society under immense delusion, delusion inevitably broken by violence, but not yet noticed as deeply broken. Their passionate nonfoundationalism that does not yield too soon to conventional history, conventional reason, or conventional church consensus is not a fad or a pet project. It is rather an urgency commensurate, in my judgment, with our current domestications of the human spirit by technological consumerism in which a chance for humanness will need to be voiced, if at all, from outside the numbness. Nonfoundationalism takes on credence and possibility — as much as it is required — when trusted universals are seen to be false, unreliable, and destructive. My question about the church before the text imagines that ours is precisely such a time as was theirs. The book with its strangeness and newness is entrusted peculiarly to such as us.

IV

From Karl Barth comes the question: "What is there in the Bible?" From Buber, from the other direction, but completely resonate with Barth: "It is the signature of our time that the spirit imposes no obligations."[25] My

25. Buber, 2.

question is the recurring one: How now does the church stand before the text and what does it do there? In an attempt to offer an answer that learns from Barth and Buber but does not simply reiterate, I make recourse to Amos Wilder. In a series of books Wilder has refused to flatten Scripture by means of historical criticism or to reduce the text to manageable proportion. Instead he insisted, in a rich variety of ways, upon the poetic, mythic, imaginative power of the text that would not be tamed to commonsense empiricism. In his 1976 book *Theopoetic,* Wilder explored the role of the artistic in biblical interpretation. Among many other things that received attention in his remarkable book, he judged:

It is true that if we look at the New Testament history in an anachronistic way we seem to see a movement devoted to soul-saving, indifferent to politics, slavery, and other social patterns. But actually it was a guerilla operation which undermined social authority by profound persuasions. What no overt force could do it did by spiritual subversion at the level of the social imagination of the polis and the provinces of the empire.[26]

In a way that I trust is faithful to Wilder's imagery of "guerilla operation" as the clue to nonfoundational intentionality to the biblical text, I want to consider the posture of "guerilla operation" when the church in our society stands before the text. Looking behind the text to the social reality of the church, Wilder comments:

Early Christianity was more like guerilla theater than social revolution, but it overthrew principalities and powers. When Jesus drove out the money changers they were no doubt back again the next day or the next week. But the episode was an acted parable and evoked the powerful theocratic vision of the prophets. . . . It was a case of liturgy against liturgy, of myth against myth. And these liturgies and myths had their institutional embodiments.[27]

26. Amos Niven Wilder, *Theopoetic: Theology and the Religious Imagination* (Philadelphia: Fortress, 1976), 28.

27. Wilder, *Theopoetic,* 28; see also Wilder, *Jesus' Parables and the War of Myths: Essays on Imagination in the Scripture* (London: SPCK, 1982).

Following Wilder, I suggest that the worship-proclamation-study space of the congregation can be reclaimed and represented precisely as theater. The preacher, moreover, can be understood as a practitioner of "guerilla theater." I suppose that I am only naming what we do, at our best, intuitively. There is, however, a gain in explicit naming and in reflecting upon what has been named.

Taking up Wilder's rich, suggestive imagery of "guerilla theater," I want to consider in turn the phrasing *theater* and then *guerilla*. On "theater" I appeal to the work of Hans Urs von Balthasar, the purpose of which is to think with you about *alternative enactment* of the *world* to the practice of faith.[28] As you may know, von Balthasar was a mystical Catholic theologian, belatedly a cardinal, a continuing dialogue partner of Karl Barth. One of the remarkable culminations of von Balthasar's work is his multi-volume study of "Theo-Drama," theological dramatic theory.[29] Von Balthasar is a theological thinker of immense erudition. While the casting of his work is unfamiliar to a Reformed Christian, attention will be usefully paid. Of course, I have not yet digested all that he says of theater — who can? I call attention to several notations in his work, while keeping in purview the categories of Erving Goffman and Kenneth Burke — and less directly Victor Turner and Clifford Geertz — and our question of the church before the text.

In his study of the interface of *faith* and *theater*, von Balthasar takes his

28. By way of situating the theological work of von Balthasar, preliminary mention should be made of the work on theater by Erving Goffman, *Frame Analysis: An Essay on Organization of Experience* (Cambridge: Harvard University Press, 1974); the extensive work of Kenneth Burke, on which see esp. *A Grammar of Motives* (Englewood Cliffs: Prentice-Hall, 1945); *A Rhetoric of Motives* (New York: Prentice-Hall, 1950); *The Rhetoric of Religion: Studies in Logology* (Berkeley: University of California Press, 1970); and the critical reflection of William H. Rueckert, *Kenneth Burke and the Drama of Human Relations* (Minneapolis: University of Minnesota Press, 1963); and James W. Chesebro, ed., *Extension of the Burkean Gesture* (Tuscaloosa: University of Alabama Press, 1993); Victor Turner, *From Ritual to Theatre: The Human Seriousness of Play* (New York: Performing Arts Journal, 1982); Clifford Geertz, *Interpretation of Cultures* (New York: Basic Books, 1973); and Peter L. Berger and Thomas Luckmann, *The Social Construction of Reality: A Treatise in the Sociology of Knowledge* (Garden City: Doubleday, 1966). Note esp. Burke's dictum, "We get our view of deeds as facts from our sense of words as facts, rather than vice versa"; *Permanence and Change: An Anatomy of Purpose*, 3rd ed. (Berkeley, University of California Press, 1984), xx.

29. Hans Urs von Balthasar, *Theo-drama: Theological Dramatic Theory* (San Francisco: Ignatius, 1988-1998).

beginning of "world as stage" from the rendering of the ancient Greeks, who of course early on dramatized lived reality. He carries his analysis through "Jewish Theater" with reference to Job, and moves then to the great drama of redemption whereby God's life in the world and for the world is lived out in the gospel. Three comments strike me as important:

First, von Balthasar carries this analysis of gospel drama precisely to the meaning of the Eucharist and its drama of God's self-giving and self-emptying.[30] Of course, a "representation" of redemption in performance will make a good Calvinist wince, fearing the "repetition" of the sacrifice. Balthasar understands the drama of salvation not simply as a past act but as an act made present in and through performance. Whether our Reformed formulations can be fully open to the dramatic dimension of sacrament, there is no doubt that it is so experienced in the church. The drama of Eucharist intimately alludes to, references, and mediates the ancient drama of crucifixion and resurrection that carries the mystery of our rescue by God. The drama is reiterated, every time, with fresh power and dramatic compulsion.

Second, in speaking of baroque theater, an aspect of his review of Christian theater, he observes:

Where existence is directly interpreted as theatre, the "I" must be understood as the role. The latter is bound to be hopelessly ambiguous, whether the world stage . . . is seen as the serious presence of a divine commission or as its symbolization, fraught with illusion: in the former case the "I" must insert itself entirely into the role . . . if it is to be itself; in the latter, it must see through it and place its center of gravity in the eternal, lest it succumb to the role.[31] But the baroque theater that vacillates between the two aspects with the result that the relationship between the "I" and the role is never ascertain-

---

30. Von Balthasar's "single drama" is as large as heaven and earth. But, of course, it pivots on christological claims that are re-enacted concretely in Eucharist. See esp. *Theo-Drama*, 4: *The Action* (San Francisco: Ignatius, 1994), 389-406.

31. The refusal to decide whether the drama is "serious presence" or "symbolization fraught with illusion" is a refusal powerfully present in the work of Goffman and Burke. See the same problematic so well voiced by Paul Ricoeur on the relation of narrative to fiction, "The Bible and Imagination," *Figuring the Sacred: Religion, Narrative, and Imagination* (Minneapolis: Fortress, 1995), 144-49; see Mark I. Wallace in his introduction to the same volume, 10-15.

able and "our masks do not sit as we would like them to". "Representation" means both showing and concealing; anyone who aspires to it must renounce his unique personality.[32]

Third, von Balthasar has stunningly observed:

> It is not insignificant that, in 1918, the year [Georg] Simmel died, and in the following year, one of the strangest phenomena of "acausal contemporaneity" in the history of the intellect took place. This was the simultaneous emergence of the "dialogue principle" in thinkers who could not be farther apart.[33]

Von Balthasar refers, in that simultaneous emergence, to Ferdinand Ebner, Martin Buber, Gabriel Marcel, and Franz Rosenzweig. In a way that anticipates Emmanuel Levinas, these thinkers saw, in a profound act against foundationalism, that reality is essentially a transaction that biblical scholars are wont to term "covenant."[34]

From this it follows, I suggest, that performance of "covenant" is a piece of theater in which the players assume roles vis-à-vis each other and in their interaction generate social reality that did not exist until that moment of dramatic exchange. In the further development of this imagery, von Balthasar moves in an explicitly theological direction, placing Jesus and the church's christological claims at the center of the single theater that matters, whereby the world is rendered new and forgiven.

Now I do not know if Amos Wilder, in his phrasing "guerilla theater," had all in mind suggested by Goffman, Burke, Turner, Geertz, and von Balthasar regarding theater. In any case, I suggest that the development of Wilder's notion of theater in that direction is useful. In antifoundationalism, this way of theological practice focuses not on settled *essences* but on dynamic *transactions* that are generative of new social reality, reality that did not exist before or apart from the transaction. And

---

32. Hans Urs von Balthasar, *Theo-Drama*, 1: *Prolegomena* (San Francisco: Ignatius, 1988), 173.

33. Von Balthasar, *Theo-Drama* 1:626.

34. The use of the term "covenant" here is not to be understood according to the recent thin constructions of criticism under the impetus of George Mendenhall, on which see Ernest W. Nicholson, *God and His People: Covenant and Theology in the Old Testament* (Oxford: Oxford University Press, 1986).

while such anti-essentialism will make some nervous and will seem to some dangerously subjective and unbearably relativistic, every pastor knows of those who hang on by their fingernails from one such dramatic enactment to the next. In such dramatic, dialogical exchanges, new participants embrace and enact the defining drama of emancipation and reconcilation, an embrace and enactment now made fully present and credible, emancipation and reconciliation now received as they have not been until this textual performance.

Wilder is not precise in his judgment about the "story of Jesus."[35] He clearly refers not to the theater of Jesus but to the theater of the text, whereby the script of Jesus continues, through the church's re-enactment, to generate a new world. This hint of church as reperformance of dramatic text is made explicit in the recent analysis of the book of Jeremiah by Louis Stulman.[36] Staying inside the text of Jeremiah itself, Stulman considers:

> We are perhaps on safest ground to think in terms of historical recontextualizations moving on a trajectory that hurtles us through space (in Palestine, Babylon, and perhaps even Egypt) and time (from the end of the seventh century to as late as the fourth century BCE). . . . The Jeremiah traditum was recast to address the matrix of needs and focal concerns, as well as the imaginative possibility of subsequent communities. Accordingly, the book was involved in a long and varied process of transmission in which the authoritative tradition was reperformed and recontextualized for a variety of social settings. These reperformances and recontextualizations of Jeremiah, however, were not extraneous or subsequent to the canonical process but in fact reflect the canonical functions of a developing sacred text in the life of the community.[37]

My reason for citing Stulman is to consider the notion of theater as a generative social interaction that yields a newly revealed world. In that context:

• I would not defend all of the claims for "role" made by Erving Goffman . . . except to notice that in the theater of the text the church and

---

35. See Amos N. Wilder, "Story and Story-World," Int 37 (1983): 353-64.

36. Louis Stulman, Order Amid Chaos: Jeremiah as Symbolic Tapestry. Biblical Seminar 57 (Sheffield: Sheffield Academic, 1998).

37. Stulman, 168-70.

its pastors take roles. Indeed, our growth in faith consists in the capacity of text-given roles occupying more of our energy and identity.

- I would not insist with Kenneth Burke that theater comprehends all . . . except to notice that theater is perhaps the only chance for life outside the shriveled world of shut-down where there is no opening of revelatory script by text.
- I would not subscribe to all that von Balthasar says . . . except that lean, didactic Protestantism may be in the process of relearning, yet again, about the defining power of sacrament that revives all of life.
- And finally, I follow Stulman . . . except to notice that the project of reperformance is not concluded by the end of the book of Jeremiah; rather, the practice of *reperformance* continues beyond the edge of the book (beyond Stulman's horizon) by the community that continues to read and hear this text and to receive its offer of another world.

I have taken so much time and effort with this matter of theater in order to return to the Ark narrative . . . and any other text upon which one might focus. The Ark narrative, whatever else it is, is *theater*. It represents a dramatic world that has the invisible but active YHWH as a key player, cast sequentially in roles of humiliation and exaltation. While the "history" at Ashdod may have concerned the Philistines, the reperformance as text surely concerns the Israelites, a vigorous dramatization that the world cannot be properly discerned apart from a God who can be captured in humiliating weakness, apart from a God who acts in self-glorifying exaltation to renovate all power relations. It is this Character, cast in this role, who destabilizes all other roles in the narrative. Surely the performance means to recruit its spectators into like roles . . . destabilized, humiliated, and exalted. Theater breaks *denial, despair,* and *complacency* in a vigorous attestation to the redefining role of YHWH.

V

I come now to Amos Wilder's second term, "guerilla," not just "theater," but "guerilla theater." Take "guerilla" as "a small band of soldiers that harass the enemy in occupied territories by surprise raids, particularly by attacking supply lines." The accent is on surprise; it is a surprise that is essentially subversive, in a manner that is perceived to be at least potentially violent. It is, moreover, aimed at the lifelines of the ammunition and supplies; it aims to cut off the sources of vitality of a power arrangement it judges to be unjust and intolerable. Wilder's usage suggests that the teaching of Jesus and the entire Jesus movement were exactly such an agonistic subversion, designed to undermine and finally to destroy the life-worlds that the gospel has judged to be wrong, unjust, false, unacceptable, and deathly. As "theater" is likely to make us nervous with its suggestion of *fiction*, so "guerilla" is likely to make us uneasy with its *agonistic* quality. If, however, Scripture is indeed a "strange new world," not contained by or adjustable to conventional arrangements of power and meaning, then it has an intrinsic agonistic quality, even if done graciously, gently, and with compassion. It could not be otherwise, for its strangeness is an assault on all things *familiar;* and its newness is a subversion of all things *old and settled.* Thus with "guerilla," we speak of its strangeness and its newness.

As I have appealed to Erving Goffman, Kenneth Burke, and Hans Urs von Balthasar to exposit "theater," so now I appeal to James C. Scott, a Yale anthropologist.[38] Scott has analyzed the careful, intentional, and ongoing transactions in tribal society between the power elites and the peasants who can never confront established power directly but who labor intentionally, "working the system . . . to their minimum disadvantage."[39] Scott is concerned with the strategies and tactics of the peasants, but assumes that the power elites have parallel intentions and operations. Concerning peasant strategies, those who must work by hidden technique to avoid violent crushing, Scott concludes:

The existence of those who seem not to rebel is a warren of minute, individual, autonomous tactics and strategies which counter and inflect the visible facts of overall domination.[40]

38. James C. Scott, *Weapons of the Weak: Everyday Forms of Peasant Resistance* (New Haven: Yale University Press, 1987); *Domination and the Arts of Resistance: Hidden Transcripts* (New Haven: Yale University Press, 1990). On the realism of theater as concrete social practice and transformation, see John C. Bentz, *Notes for a Prophetic Theater: An Exploration of Performance as a Tool for Justice* (thesis, Gonzoga University, 2000).

39. Scott, *Weapons of the Weak*, xv. See Eric Hobsbawn, "Peasants and Politics," *Journal of Peasant Studies* 1/1 (1973): 3-22, cited by Scott.

40. Scott, *Weapons of the Weak*, vii, quotes this from Colin Gordon commenting on Michael Foucault. Scott offers no citation for Gordon's comment.

By a study of a Malaysian village, Scott identifies those strategies and tactics as "foot-dragging, dissimulation, false compliance, pilfering, feigned ignorance, slander, arson, sabotage and so forth," actions that

> require little or no coordination or planning; they often represent a form of individual self-help; and they typically avoid any direct symbolic confrontation with authority or with elite norms.[41]

While Scott has paid great attention to actions, in his second book, *Domination and the Arts of Resistance,* he has paid more attention to the coded ideology that informs and sustains ad hoc conspiracy — the ideology that is carried by "stories" and "gossip," that is "a partisan effort (by class, faction, family) to advance its claims and interests against those of others."[42] He refers to this coded ideology as a "script," a sustained, reiterated tale of identity. Of this script Scott concludes:

- The powerful and decisive script is backstage, never public.
- The peasants also have a public transcript that the elite are able to see;
- There is a wide divergence between the public and offstage scripts of the peasants.
- There is a like divergence among elites between public and offstage scripts, but the divergence is not as wide as it is for peasants.
- One cannot ascertain the offstage script from public interaction, for the offstage script is too clever and stealthy for that.
- Power relations require peasants to survive by a hidden script.

Now, in case you do not get the point, I will summarize by quoting the Ethiopian aphorism that opens Scott's second book:

> When the great lord passes by the wise peasant bows deeply, and silently farts.[43]

In his second book, Scott is more inclined to notice the evidence, not in far-off Malaysia, but closer to home in U.S. race relations. African-Americans must operate with precisely such a hidden transcript.

41. Scott, *Weapons of the Weak,* 29.
42. Scott, *Weapons of the Weak,* 23, 282.
43. Scott, *Domination and the Arts of Resistance,* frontispiece.

Moreover, Scott's second book pays attention to the dramatic moment when the hidden transcript is "for the first time" made public. Scott's classic case of such "going public" is the moment in totalitarian Romania when President Ceausescu assembled throngs in a stadium in order to exhibit, one more time, his unchallenged, haughty power.[44] As his entourage processed into the filled stadium with characteristically excessive military strutting and posturing, the Romanian peasants began to laugh and laugh and laugh; it was that public exhibit of a long secret mocking, so Scott proposes, that destroyed, in an instant, the fake claims of the abusive elite that no longer had any credibility. Thus Scott suggests that in interactive power relations, the rich and the poor, the weak and the strong, tell different tales of social reality, and in the meantime posture deceptively . . . until there is a daring moment of disclosure that changes everything. Listen again to Amos Wilder:

Actually it was a guerilla operation which undermined social authority by profound persuasions. What no overt force could do it did by spiritual subversion at the level of social imagination of the polis and the provinces of the empire.[45]

Wilder provides a clue; Scott gives it social body and force. Together Wilder and Scott, respectively, with an interest in social imagination and social power, suggest to me a way of understanding the church's practice of the text. The text is the hidden transcript of the faithful, the offstage lore of the people of God in the world who hold tenaciously to a countervision of reality. That countervision, it can be easily argued, was generated from below in terms of socio-economic location; but, of course, that countervision can indeed be held by the powerful as well who refuse to sign on with the dominant claims that appear most appropriate to their social location.

Every preacher knows that the work of countervision cannot be done very frontally, but must be done mostly by stealth. But what if we imagine the church meeting with the text as the practice of the "backstage transcript," the secret commitment held by the faithful that can hardly be ut-

44. Scott, *Domination and the Arts of Resistance*, 204-5. See the editorial comment on the spectacular event, London *Times*, December 23, 1999.

45. Amos Wilder, *Theopoetic*, 28.

tered credibly in the presence of the manor lord or at City Hall or at Nike headquarters? The secret transcript is not secret because it is gnostic or mysterious, but because it is dangerous and revolutionary, or as Barth proposed, "strange and new." The utterance remains mostly hidden because one must count the cost of going public. The hidden transcript is characteristically "strange and new" in cadences that dazzle, upset, and reassure:

A wandering Aramean was my father. . . .

In the year that King Uzziah died, I saw the king. . . .

Woe to those who join house to house. . . .

Do not remember former things. . . .

Vanity of vanity, all is vanity. . . .

Those who mock the poor insult their Maker. . . .

Blessed are those who do not walk in the way of the wicked. . . .

I saw a new heaven and a new earth. . . .

I am sure that neither life nor death. . . .

In the same night in which he was betrayed. . . .

He was raised on the third day, according to the scriptures . . .

Husbands, love your wives as Christ loved the church. . . .

God did not give us a spirit of cowardice. . . .

Dip in almost anywhere. The utterances, of course, claim to be grounded; they are, however, public utterances, uttered out of the blue, grounded in what the world does not credit. They are utterances that assault our closely held worlds. They are surprise raids, surprise assaults on imagination, surprise every time uttered and every time heard, raids that expose the limited ammunition of the rulers of this age, attacks that cut off the supply lines and the oxygen lines of easier ways in the world. They cut the communication lines to other resources by suggesting that the other modes of communication have missed the news. They expose the supply lines we counted on by making clear that the genuine sources of life are other than we had thought.

And then public! Public occasionally on the great issues of the day when the emergency is so deeply felt that it cannot be hidden any longer.

Public when the community of stealth is schooled enough in courage to stand by its hidden transcript when it goes "onstage." There comes a break of irreverence in which new assertion breaks the world. There is a public weeping over the world that has died before our very eyes, even while the Super Bowls of consumerism have their day; there is an Easter laugh in which the community of this script is undaunted and unafraid and so sure of the future yet to be given.

What the church does when it stands before the text, I propose, is that it engages in *theater;* it entertains an alternative. It trusts, moreover, that its theater is rooted in trusted reality that remains unproven and unprovable, grounded in no available universal and in no measured historicity. It trusts that this "theater" will undermine, expose, and subvert old truth held too long that smells of denial, despair, and death. It knows on a good day of this other script, hidden but laden with life, hidden, guarded, but bursting with newness that the world must know. When the church risks that other text, hidden and then abruptly public, it proclaims what "has been hidden from the foundation of the world" (Matt. 13:35), "destined before the foundation of the world, but was revealed at the end of the days for your sake" (1 Pet. 1:20). Those realities are operative, I propose, wittingly or not, every time the church stands before the text.

So consider:

- from Amos Wilder, the phrase "guerilla theater." For all his interest in rhetoric and art, Wilder here still makes a statement that is historical and sociological. I depart enough from Wilder to talk not only about the Jesus movement of early Christianity, but also about the ongoing use of the text in the continued work of guerilla theater;
- from Hans Urs von Balthasar, the notion of theater as an interactive practice of reality that refuses monologue, taking the "theater" out of his dense historical analysis to see that the reperformance of the text generates alternative reality, strange and new;
- from James C. Scott, who witnesses to counterreality scripts that in stealth and subversion do constitute revolutionary, transformative guerilla action.

From Wilder, von Balthasar, and Scott I weave together a hermeneutic of "guerilla theater." Under this rubric we retain the large question of what the church does when it stands before the text. But then we keep it simple and concrete by returning to the particularity of the Ark narrative with its candor that refuses *denial*, with its glory that refuses *despair*, and with its holiness that refuses *complacency* in the telling of God. The Ark narrative, then, I take as a representative practice of the church, as guerilla theater, as a hidden script of lore told among those "peasants" who subscribe to an alternative casting of social reality.

There is a clue about the social location of the narrative in 1 Sam. 13:19-21. Israel was a disadvantaged community that lived in part by the permit of the Philistines:

> Now there was no smith to be found throughout all the land of Israel; for the Philistines said, "The Hebrews must not make swords or spears for themselves"; so all the Israelites went down to the Philistines to sharpen their plowshare, mattocks, axes, or sickles; The charge was two-thirds of a shekel for the plowshares and for the mattocks, and one-third of a shekel for sharpening the axes and for setting the goads. So on the day of the battle neither sword nor spear was to be found in the possession of any of the people with Saul and Jonathan.

And then the narrative adds, enigmatically:

> but Saul and his son Jonathan had them. (v. 22)

They had no weapons. They had no chance against the superior technology of the Philistines who are always careful not to let the most recent military technology fall into the hands of the unreliable who may turn foe. They had no chance.

But we are, following Scott, considering "The Weapons of the Weak." Perhaps they met regularly, gossiping, as Deborah says, "at the watering places" (Judg. 5:10-11) . . . or wherever . . . to tell the story the Philistines would not believe. It is a story that they themselves could hardly believe, that must be kept secret in its threat, but must be told to the young. So they said, "Tell of it, you who ride, you who sit, you who walk, tell it all the time.[46] But not a peep to the Philistines."

---

46. On the cruciality of this text, see Brueggemann, *Theology of the Old Testament*, 130-32.

Not new stories, but stories known and loved best;[47] among them, treasured and repeated, remembered and hoped, is this tale of Eli and Ichabod and Dagon and the ark and the God who sits on the ark and rides home in glory.

- They told the tale true *against denial:* YHWH was indeed captured!
- They told the tale bold *against despair:* something happened unseen in the night that changed everything, beyond explanation.
- They told the tale to the end, without apology. No ground for *complacency,* even when come home; this home-coming, home-bringing God remains dangerous and beyond grasp.

They told the tale true and bold and clear to the end. They told the tale centered in this Character who is captured unexpectedly and then is broken free inexplicably. The visible residue from the tale is a god with his arms broken, lying on the threshold, quietly supine and gladly submissive. If you do not believe it, you can go to Ashdod and still see the silly priests step ostentatiously over the doorsill, an old superstition that betokens Dagon's shame and YHWH's recovered glory (1 Sam. 5:5). They told the tale of a partisan power committed on their behalf. They did not worry about other weapons like swords and spears; they did not lose nerve or accept diminishment by an unresponsive military technology. They told the story and waited, all the time haunted, a story so incredible that in-laws may have doubts, but told with its waiting and its haunting, watching the glory regularly headed home.

It is *theater,* a drama that shows and conceals. It is *guerilla,* a hidden raid of surprise. It is *guerilla theater* and we count it canon. We gather round it. Some are charged to tell it again. Sometimes the story does its work. It rushes to the hiddenness in order to confirm the hope that can hardly be uttered, so weary are we of the Philistines. It impacts the children who are always in the contest between stories. It reaches out with power and meets the crypto-Philistines who are situated in the covenant community, and jars when we listen. It shocks, it stuns, it invites, it buoys; all are free to imagine that the world is indeed this way and not some other. The

47. See Wilder, *Int* 37 (1983): 353-64; and more generally, Stanley Hauerwas and L. Gregory Jones, eds., *Why Narrative? Readings in Narrative Theology* (Grand Rapids: Wm. B. Eerdmans, 1989).

teller is cunning, not risking too much, until there is a public moment when all must be risked. And then the truth is told, cast as public theology, insisting that those outside the secret should also notice the possibility long hidden and now visible.

VI

I have tried to frame this retelling from Ashdod in the most non-foundational way I know. Some among us, no doubt confirmed foundationalists with deep confidence in old universals, will find such an effort foolish and unpersuasive. But then, this dangerous, hidden transcript is not for those who still trust the old universals and who believe that the established elites know best and, in any case, have all the jobs on offer. No need for such a story among them. My burden in these lectures is to insist that for the church and its pastors to have a new word to speak — in a context not unlike these beset Israelites or in a context like the small "raiding parties" of early disciples — a word new and strange is most likely to arise from "the strange new world of the Bible."

In a clumsy way I have urged this nonfoundational enterprise in my theology, with responses one might expect. I want to locate myself specifically in the current conversation, in order that we may think well and clearly about nonfoundational claims for the text in the church. I will do this by considering important and serious critiques of my work that I will cleverly label A, B, and C:[48]

A is for Anderson, Bernhard Anderson, beloved Princeton teacher. In his recent and elegant Old Testament theology, *Contours of Old Testament Theology,* Anderson uses some pages to critique my "extreme" treatment of "historical claims," for as he says, biblical faith cannot do without history.[49] The problem, of course, is that "history" means many things, and one has not accomplished very much at all by insisting upon "history." Let us consider the "historical" question of the Ark narrative. The most that Patrick Miller and J. J. M. Roberts can do is to cite parallels to the capture

48. For what follows, see my article, "The ABC's of Old Testament Theology in the US," *ZAW* (forthcoming).

49. Bernhard W. Anderson, *Contours of Old Testament Theology* (Minneapolis: Fortress, 1999).

and release of cultic icons. All right so far. But, of course, that is not what the text claims or asserts. One cannot find "objective" evidence for this particular capture and release of a cultic icon; but even if one could, that is not what concerns the text. What the text says is that "early in the morning" they saw the residue of what had hiddenly transpired in the night. The important point is completely hidden from historical analysis . . . as is the rescue of the exiles from Babylon, as is the release from Egypt, as is the Easter of new life. We cannot say what "happened" . . . unless, of course, we take the text as true testimony. Without this true testimony, there is no "happening." But when taken as true there is ample happening. It is deep foundationalism to imagine [sic] that the crucial turns of the Bible match the universal claims of recoverable "historicity." The hidden transcript of Israel never traffics in universal claims, but always knows better in hidden ways.

Anderson himself, moreover, knows that "history" as an interpretive category is deeply problematic. This is not the Anderson who taught at Princeton 35 years ago and who in *Understanding* stayed very close to the archaeological line of William Foxwell Albright and of G. Ernest Wright, to whom his book is dedicated. This is a more sobered Anderson who, like almost all of us, now knows that "history" is constituted as an infrastructure of image, metaphor, narrative, and imagination that proposes a world to us some distance from any recoverable "fact." What is given is in some great measure an advocacy, perhaps an imperial advocacy or a protesting alternative.[50] The happenedness of this wonder at Ashdod is not doubted; but it is given in a hidden certitude that will not be measured by public, Philistine historians. It is not possible, as was tried in the midst of the last century, to reconstruct knowable history and then to stir a little YHWH into it where convenient. Rather, one must take it whole from the teller of tales and then see if one's life and the life of one's community can be resituated in that telling, outside every domination, no weapons from the alien blacksmith but only the weapon of a hidden script that refuses to conform or submit.

B is for James Barr, sometime teacher at Princeton. He is an unreconstructed, untroubled foundationalist who has complete confidence in "objective" Western rationality. His polemical comments concerning my book

---

50. This point has been especially effectively argued by Edward Said, *Orientalism* (New York: Pantheon, 1978).

are legion, but the core issue is that I do not stay firmly within the bounds Barr would set for all of us of that rationality; rather, I have engaged in the detail of the text that is prerational or even nonrational, with a sorry dose of homiletical style.[51] (He also observes, without naming names, that I have cited many "second rate" scholars, though I assume that does not refer to any of the present company, many of whom I have cited.)[52]

The problem with Barr's defense of such rationality is that he never discusses texts, certainly none as primitive as the Ark narrative, to show us what his rational objectivity might mean with reference to such a text. Judged by any modernist, Enlightenment rationality, the Ark narrative is too primitive to countenance. What could it mean that one God shoves another god in the dark stillness of the night in order to win a glorious victory and leave the body parts of the Philistine god strewn on the temple threshold? Likely Barr would say, with a modernist notion of "history," that it is just a "story."[53] Well, of course; but then, that is exactly what I have said.

The difference between us is that I have insisted that it is a story for taking seriously, for it specifies concretely the plot line and key Character of our faith. Put more bluntly, the difference is that I have said this is *a useable, important datum for faith.* Indeed, if this story is so primitive as to be "un-serious," there will be no categories left for Easter and we will end in the arid ethical insistences of the Jesus Seminar. But, of course, it is at the core of Barr's cold stricture that one cannot in principle do interpretation for the church and call it "reasonable," for such belief-ful reading skews the critical task. Barr is completely uncompromising on this point, oblivious to the fact that his own rational objectivity is itself a faith affirmation now placed in acute doubt by the steady and deep critiques of modernity. Unlike Anderson who knows that "history" has been problematized even though he wishes it had not been, Barr has no sense that Enlightenment rationality has been profoundly problematized, and makes his own authoritarian dismissal that finally must, so it seems to me, deny the seriousness of the text. Barr's polemic seems to me a curious throwback to happier days, days that are long since gone beyond recovery. His statement warrants attention, nonetheless, precisely because it is an account of how

---

51. James Barr, *The Concept of Biblical Theology* (Minneapolis: Fortress, 1999).
52. Barr, *The Concept of Biblical Theology,* 556.
53. See James Barr, "Story and History in Biblical Theology," *JR* 56 (1976): 1-17.

the church has given up on the text and settled for less dangerous categories of interpretation that turn out to be stunningly thin on energy and
courage. Rationality that excludes the "pre-rational" narrative concrete-
ness of the text has robbed the church of its most elemental energy for
mission.

In contrast to the argument of Professor Barr, my own judgment is
that such a church must return to the temple at Ashdod and see again the
pitiful priests leaping over the place where the body parts were left, a journey much too naive for Barr. For all his impatience and anger at the church
that is in his judgment much too authoritarian in its interpretive insistence, Barr leaves the question for us whether the preacher of the church
and the church before the text can enact a kind of innocence, a second
naiveté, that is twice naive without second-guessing.[54]

C is for Brevard Childs, teacher of us all. I have learned the most from
Childs of all my teachers of biblical theology of the last decades. The differences I have from his presentation are not great, but they are as important
to me as they are to him. His primary critique of my theology is that the
distinction — albeit a distinction that is clearly richly dialectical — between what I have called "core-testimony" and "counter-testimony" is unacceptable.[55] Indeed, he goes so far as to suggest that I have voiced a "gnostic" division, even though I have taken pains to show the interrelatedness
of the parts and have proceeded on the recognition that one cannot say everything at one time, even as Professor Childs in his great book of 1993
must parcel out his argument under distinct "themes."[56] In the case of the
present text, I do not know if Professor Childs would make the same judgment here; if he would not, then his critique, so it seems to me, does not
pertain with much force.

In the present narrative it is clear that in chapter 4 YHWH is captured
and defeated; in chapter 5 it is equally clear that YHWH is victorious and

54. Barr, of course, would have no interest in any naiveté, second or first or any kind.
But, of course, his passion for objective rationality leaves him in a corner, unable to make
any serious theological claim. He intends to makes such claims, but it is not clear how his
own claims (as *The Concept of Biblical Theology*, 186) relate to his objective rationality.

55. Brevard S. Childs, "Walter Brueggemann's *Theology of the Old Testament: Testimony, Dispute, Advocacy*," *SJT* 53 (2000): 228-33. See my response, "A Response to Professor
Childs," *SJT* 53 (2000): 234-38.

56. Brevard S. Childs, *Biblical Theology of the Old and New Testaments: Theological Reflection on the Christian Bible* (Minneapolis: Fortress, 1992), 349-716.

on his way home. These are, moreover, two quite distinct moves, both of which are essential to the narrative and to the God featured in the narrative. The narrator and the listening community that hears the text do not know and cannot know ahead of time, at the end of chapter 4, how the narrative will turn. Israel must at least leave open, upon hearing, that in the narrative it may meet *the captured, defeated God* or *the God victorious* and on the way home. One cannot say all these things at the same time, mainly because the narrative drama requires that they be said distinctly, properly paced, and sequenced.

I have observed, and made as much interpretive gain as I could, of the caesura between 1 Sam. 4:10-22 and 5:1-4. In the first of these texts, we have seen the defeat of YHWH by the Philistines and the capture of the ark. YHWH had set out only to destroy the priestly dynasty of Eli. YHWH, however, became so entangled in that combat that YHWH was also taken, clearly not YHWH's initial intent. By the end of that narrative section in chapter 4, YHWH is humiliated and shamed in defeat, a Philistine trophy, as the wife of Phinehas recognizes. In deep disjunction and rapid reversal, 5:1-4 inexplicably and without any curiosity narrates the return of YHWH to glory, power, and sovereignty, accompanied by the savage dismissal of Dagon, who is exposed as a fake god without power. The narrative has no interest in or strategy for relating the two points that are hinged only by moving from scene to scene. We are given quite distinct scenes of humiliation and exaltation, the exaltation being all the more glorious because the humiliation is so final and deep, the exaltation moreover beyond any expectation that the narrative in chapter 4 entertains. The distinction, contrast, and tension between the two is elemental to the movement and intent of the narrative.

Now it may be that there is no issue here with Professor Childs. I have been warned in an article by Professor Dennis Olson — not warned in a dream but in an article — that I have caricatured Childs, and I have no wish or need to do so.[57] It has appeared to me that Professor Childs has collapsed the downside of YHWH's narrative in order to make it all more splendid and certain. Against that inclination I have wanted, for textual and interpretive reasons, to let the downside have its full, unhurried say, discrete and unqualified, linked to but not itself corrected or qualified by

---

57. Dennis T. Olson, "Biblical Theology as Provisional Monologization: A Dialogue with Childs, Brueggemann and Bakhtin," *BibInt* 6 (1998): 162-80.

the upside of YHWH's sovereignty and splendor. Thus in reading and hearing this text, one must pause long — longer I believe than Professor Childs would — between 4:10-22 and 5:1-4, pause long enough to honor and notice the abyss, pause because for over a day the narrator did not know what to say next, pause to ensure that the "counter-testimony" soaks in before that "counter-testimony" is too readily or too easily countered in turn and trumped by good news. The disjunctive quality of the narrative, I have insisted, is precisely reflective of and congruent with the disjunctive dimension of YHWH's own character. That disjunction is at the heart of our hearing, and we must not read smoothly or quickly across the disjunction of counter-testimony to core-testimony.[58]

VII

My question, with reference to the Ark narrative as a case in point, is to ask, what do the church and its pastors do in front of the text. My insistence echoes the earliest Barth, because I believe that the church's evangelical claim is as urgent with the end of our known world as it was in Barth's time with the ending of his known world, albeit a very different ending of a very different world. The ending we now face is mostly covered over and not yet noticed at root, an ending of the claims of humanness upon which we have relied in dominant Western culture. What the church and its pastors do before the text is to let the text line out a strange, new world, a world new and a world strange:

- Not restrained by conventional *historical* notions of what could have happened, for this happening at Ashdod in the dark stillness of the night defies our notions of happening.[59] And certainly Professor An-

58. It may well be that the acknowledgment or disregard of the disjunction is the core issue between Professor Childs and myself. One can wonder how deep the disjunction is to be discerned in the claims of Old Testament theology, and even more crucially, whether the disjunction is only in the awarenesses of the interpretive community or whether it extends even into the very character of God. On this point, my own judgment is deeply at variance from that of Professor Childs. See Brueggemann, *Theology of the Old Testament*, 325-32; "Texts that Linger, Not Yet Overcome."

59. The peculiar criteria for the claims of distinctive "historical" happening are noted generically by W. B. Gallie, "The Historical Understanding," in *History and Theory*, ed. George H.

derson, for all his insistence upon "history," could not go very far toward explicating the "happenedness" of this narrative, nor would
most scholars with such an interest do much more "historical" with
this text than the cultic model offered by Miller and Roberts that is inescapably silent on what "happened."

• Not restrained by inherited Enlightenment notions of *rationality*, for
the turn in the narrative is a deep irrationality for which the night provides the required cover. The narrative quite deliberately refuses the
"Enlightened rationality" preferred by Professor Barr, for nothing here
makes any sense, given the modern reasonableness which he champions; indeed, Barr's categories allow nothing of the hidden struggle of
the gods that leads to an inscrutable beheading and disarming. It is exactly the inscrutable beyond explanation to which Professor Barr
strenuously objects.

• Not restrained by a conventional *canonical* reading that trims the
edges of this God, manifestly defeated, stunningly victorious — all accomplished in the nighttime disjunction of narrative utterance — in
order to make things fit without an unbearable and unmanaged and
therefore unpredictable disjunction.

This text we call "Scripture," that we take as gospel carrier, to which we
"listen for the word of God," is an offer of a world strange and new, unre-
strained by our accommodationist habits that want the text to meet *historical* expectation, *Enlightenment rationality*, or even the *centrist confession* of
the church. The preacher's glorious task is to handle texts that refuse all of
these accommodations, that lead us to holiness that destroys asnd creates.

I do not know if Anderson, Barr, or Childs would countenance Amos
Wilder's category of "guerilla theater," or Kenneth Burke's conviction that
"the play's the thing," or James Scott's discernment of a "hidden transcript" among the powerless that is offstage but occasionally comes disrup-
tively onstage. I only suggest that our habitual ways of reading and hearing
have too much thinned the strangeness and the newness of the text, even
as Reformed people remain convinced that energy for mission derives precisely from the strangeness and newness of the text.

Nadel (Middletown: Wesleyan University Press, 1977), 149-202; and more specifically by Richard Reinhold Niebuhr, *Resurrection and Historical Reason: A Study of Theological Method* (New
York: Scribner's, 1957).

So consider:

• The Ark narrative is *theater;* it is an act of imagination that, in the words of Northrup Frye, is "to take a sabbatical from our commitments."[60] That is why we go to the theater: to ponder and wonder if it could be "otherwise."[61] The conventional assumption in that ancient world, shared by Philistines and Israelites, was that the Philistines had power and technology and Israel was fated to be subservient. For those who cared about theological extrapolation from the "facts on the ground," Dagon was evidently superior and devotees of YHWH must be careful and deferential in appropriate ways. Yahwists must be careful to "tell it not in Gath" (see 2 Sam. 1:20), that is, not give any more data to support Philistine arrogance. So the Israelites — and this God? — knuckled under, kept their heads down and their mouths shut. But then came this utterance of alternative that functioned immediately as new social fact among Israelites. The text is precisely that uttered alternative which, when taken up as social fact, changes everything. The alternative utterance is new and strange and it yields, for those who take up its construal, a world strange and new.

In this uttered alternative, Dagon has power only until sundown. In the alternative, after sundown when the priests had turned out the lights, things happened, strange and new things. There was a power loose in Dagon's own house beyond the control of Dagon or his priests. The power was exercised in a jab and a left hook, a nightly vigor, and perhaps a gloating grin that would be curbed and sobered by sunrise. And the silly priests continue to hop over the threshold filled with broken body parts.

It is only theater. But it is, in fact, *guerilla theater.* This is a surprise attack, an act of narrative performance that undermines and subverts and shows differently. As close as we usually come to such enacted subversion of our assumed givens is in the coded "spirituals" of "Negro slaves" who sang of a difference that the master class did not recognize as subversive, or in Minjung theology in Korea, whereby power is mocked in ways that are unrecognized by the overlords, unrecognized until it is

60. Northrup Frye, *The Critical Path* (Bloomington: Indiana University Press, 1971), 171.
61. See Walter Brueggemann, "The Faithfulness of 'Otherwise'" (forthcoming).

too late.[62] The drama of our narrative is for the Israelites first, perhaps Israelite peasants who had access to none of the technology; the matter dawns on the Philistine overlords only later, always too late:

They sent therefore and gathered together all the lords of the Philistines, and said, "Send away the ark of the God of Israel, and let it return to its own place, that it may not kill us and our people." (1 Sam. 5:11)

This YHWH, they learned late and in distress, cannot be safely held (see Acts 2:24). This YHWH cannot be held at all. Here and there, over the course of time, over the course of many narrative performances, it dawned on Israel that if this God is not held, neither can God's people be held. And the Philistines belatedly noticed that if the God of Israel goes free, then the Israelites will go free . . . politically, economically, culturally. The ultimate irony is that through its emancipation enacted in subversive drama, there is an exuberance for Israel but an assault upon the Philistines; the powerful are placed in jeopardy and the powerless are on their way rejoicing; the map of human reality is drastically rearranged in the utterance of the text (see Luke 6:20-25) — all of that as an act of imagination,

- not curbed by a generic idea of *history;*
- not dismissed by a conventional assertion of *rationality;*
- not tamed by a smoothed *canon* of faith,

but set there in all its textual disjunctiveness as testimony to this most dis-junctive of all Holiness.

The tale, as a piece of guerilla theater, is so enigmatic and empowering, so strange and new, that the children of these first hearers put the narrative in their sacred book for reuse. It cannot, however, be reused if it is curbed by history or if it is dismissed by reason or if it is tamed by canon. It must be let be as it is, new and strange.

And so, belatedly, are its reusers, we church and we pastors, also in-vited to be uncurbed, undismissed, and untamed in this strangeness and this newness, all given in narrative utterance. So imagine, text time on

---

62. See, representatively, Kim Yong Bock, ed., *Minjung Theology: People as the Subjects of History,* rev. ed. (Maryknoll: Orbis, 1983).

Sunday morning (or whenever), 15 Episcopalians or 20 Presbyterians or 40 Baptists engaged in theatrical subverting. In the listening company recruited by this text are those who have never been to Ashdod. They know, however, about captivity, failure, and powerlessness. They wait for somebody to tell the candid truth about powerlessness. They pause to see if anyone can fill the dark stillness with new power. They listen in "Silent Night, Holy Night" to see if holiness will break upon their illness, their failed families, their devouring economy, their fresh sense of mortality, their ache for worlds lost, their wretchedness in a world too palpable. Some ask, some challenge, some deny, some keep their heads down. And then consider that the guerilla forces say, "Listen one more time." Listen about the candor of captivity and the surprise of emancipation. Watch all the silly priests and notice the cows headed East with the cart. The text that defies *history*, challenges *reason*, and strains *canon* is for reusing — many times. That reusing I will take up as our work in our final exploration together.

HAVE A NICE WEEKEND

Thus far I have considered the Ark narrative as it might be said and heard in a nonfoundationalist reading, that is, heard without being curbed by the limitations of accommodating, universal requirements, whether of "history," "reason," or "canon." I have suggested that such a concrete and particular reading is appropriate and necessary in the church precisely in a time when so-called universals are exposed as interested and partial and when they squeeze the particular to nonexistence. It may well be that a fresh concrete and particular reading will contribute to the formulation of fresh ways of the universal, but that is not known ahead of time. Such a particular reading, however, cannot wait on the assurance of a pending universal.

I

In such a reading that is more-or-less (never fully) unencumbered, I have paid particular attention to the dramatic movement of the narrative that stretches over three days:

- *Day one:* a day of defeat, capture, and humiliation;
- *Day two:* a day of hidden combat; and
- *Day three:* a day of release, the third day that stretches into seven months, on which see 6:1.

The dramatic sequence insists on each scene being taken discretely and seriously, in order to exhibit the God who dominates the narrative development, a God vulnerable and defenseless, a God powerful and assertive, a God triumphant and not to be trifled with, not even by the closest adherents of this God. This narrative of three days, moreover, is a script for "guerilla theater," an endlessly available re-enactment, retelling, rehearing, redescribing, reperformance that issues a surprise reading against every settled human world. The narrative invites Israel:

- out of *denial* that imagines an endlessly triumphant God;
- out of *despair* that imagines an endlessly defeated God;
- out of *complacency* that imagines a returned God as a house pet.

The subversive *theater* of this script affirms to Israel that the claims of Philistine domination — in part accepted by Israel — are a false portrayal of reality. The *guerilla* aspect of the narrative intends to subvert the domesticated imagination of Israel, making a bid that Israel should entertain a very different world of assurance and danger that centers in the character of YHWH. The script lines out the utterances Israel is to make in each new performance, and even goes so far as to provide the lines that need to be uttered by the Philistines, good Yahwistic theologians that they are, in order to keep the plot going (see 4:7-8; 6:6).

The narrative does not seem to object if the Philistines stand at the end of the crowd of Israelites to watch the subversive performance, here and there finding their hegemonic world delegitimated, perchance to come over to Israel and its God.[1] The bid to the Philistines made by the narrative, however, is secondary; the first intended audience is surely the Israelites who have long recited the Exodus narrative, but who are perhaps numbed to its durable persuasive force. A fresh performance of a new text may be a way to enliven the recital of the old text that may be too easily mouthed but not noticed. My reading of the Ark narrative thus far yields a subversive three-day drama, a sequenced portrayal that eventuates in an offer of a counterreality, counter to the dominant reality that consistently robs Israel of its faith, its freedom, and its courage.

---

1. On the outsider who may listen in and join, see Walter Brueggemann, *Biblical Perspectives on Evangelism: Living in a Three-Storied Universe* (Nashville: Abingdon, 1993), 48-70.

II

It was the thought of a three-day sequence that led me to the title of this lecture. I tried to think of another three-day sequence that might illuminate this three-day offer of counterreality. Asking about three-day sequences led me, as a foil, to "the weekend." About as close as we get to a secular blessing in our society is, "Have a nice weekend," a wish for a significant, self-focused break in a routine world of work that is itself thought to be without significance.

The weekend as a social institution and practice is enormously powerful and pervasive among us. In an acknowledgment of its power and importance, increasing numbers of businesses now permit "dressing down" on Friday, rather like "weekend eve," a time of preparation. I understand, as well, that what used to be the uncurbed practice of Friday night drinking on college campuses has largely moved to Thursday night, in order not to interrupt the sacred time of the weekend with its endless round of sports, entertainment, shopping, and homecoming, all formats of self-indulgence underwritten by consumer ideology. The weekend as social institution and practice is an occasion of privatistic escape, freedom of responsibilities (though allowing for Saturday "chores"), engaged as though there were no human issues before us, no large public questions of violence and deprivation, and no antidotes requiring a response of serious, engaged passion. It is an occasion of escapist stillness, devoid of the jarring rough and tumble of narrative interaction. It goes without saying that the social institution and practice of weekend is enormously difficult for the conventional church; nonetheless the weekend is so authoritative and attractive that serious church believers, like everyone else, flee to the mountains or the shore or wherever as soon and as often as possible. It is evidently an article of consumer faith that the goal of life is to escape the tribulations.

When the battle at Aphek was joined, when Israel was routed and the ark was captured, when YHWH was taken captive to the Philistine temple, with Dagon serenely enthroned in the stillness of his temple, one can imagine the priests and leading citizens of Ashdod, about to go home triumphant, gathered in a liturgy for which the litany went like this:

Now we have won . . . have a nice weekend;
Now Dagon is victorious . . . have a nice weekend;

121

Now YHWH is subjugated . . . have a nice weekend;
Now the Israelites are routed . . . have a nice weekend;
Dagon be with you . . . and also with you;
Have a nice weekend!

For this assembly there is no unfinished business. Not to worry. These people have no narrative, no drama that disrupts, no living Character who stirs among them. They have no real theater, because there is no new disclosing, no guerilla action, because they intend nothing to be subverted. All is well and all is well and all will be well. Well, perhaps this is an overstated caricature; but then Israel's narrative, with its subversive lead Character, regularly evokes caricature and overstatement.

III

The banishment of dangerous narrative and the substitution of predictable mantras result in a narcotic for the weekend crowd. It would be so even in Israel, except that Israel has narratives that will not be reduced and that insist upon their jarring, endlessly jarring, retelling. The three-day deal — on the weekend or anytime — is very different for people who are embedded in a narrative that revolves around real issues in a sequence with a Holy Character. The narrative mode of presentation disrupts and differentiates time, sequences action, and permits plot development that continues long after the story itself has ended; the lights do not go out on the key Character, regardless of what Dagon may think. I thought about this three-day narrative and the three-day weekend, and I judge that communities with narratives of three days are summoned and reassured differently from those who have no such three-day narrative:

• a three-day deal that pivots on Friday prayer *(Salat al-Jum'ah)* for Muslims;
• a three-day deal that pivots on Sabbath for Jews,
• and most especially for the present company, a three-day deal that pivots on Easter Sunday for Christians.

All these communities are people of the book, or perhaps better, people of the script. People of the narrative, moreover, tell and hear their lives differently from the textless, narrative-deprived people of the weekend who substitute privatized commodity for engaging, disruptive drama. Obviously, the three communities of this text are not precisely symmetrical; nonetheless, all share together against the ideology of the weekend the dreadful, wondrous timefulness of the narrative.

IV

A nonfoundational or even anti-foundational reading such as I propose — against the constraints of universalizing categories — attends to the particularity of the text. Such a reading does not, however, leave the church — or its preachers — with only the thin critical analysis of the text in which we are all so well schooled. A nonfoundational reading that eschews external restraints may attest to the *internal thickness* of the text. It does so by two characteristic strategies.

First, it reads the text *intertextually,* recognizing that this text lives in the presence of many other texts in the textual horizon of the community of faith.[2] It receives from and contributes to other texts that cannot be arranged in any chronological sequence; it alludes to other, antecedent texts and is taken up as allusion by other derivative texts. When we attend to the intertextual process, we notice, inevitably I believe, that the characteristic and extreme practices of historical criticism have largely resisted such inner textual reference to our great disadvantage; but against such rationalistic thinning we also know well that no serious text community reads in the way in which we have been mostly schooled.

Second, on the basis of an *intertextual reading* that is *nonfoundational,* that is, uncurbed by external restraints, the text is *reread* and is heard to *remean* in the presence of other texts that are available in the rich memory and the present recital of the community. In our case, thus, the Ark narrative does not stand isolated simply as an account of an ancient Philistine encounter. We are, rather, on the basis of intertextual allusion, permitted to reread the text in the larger embedment to which Israel attends and on which it relies. In what follows, I will undertake three rereadings of the Ark narrative, each of which seeks at the same time to

---

2. The normative discussion of intertextuality is by Michael Fishbane, *Biblical Interpretation in Ancient Israel* (Oxford: Oxford University Press, 1985).

take the text in its deep particularity and to take it "at large" in the imagination of Israel.[3]

My first rereading is based on the astonishing connections to 2 Isaiah
that have accrued in my discussion.[4] I did not begin with such an awareness, but have been amazed and reassured by the dense correspondence.
The first day of the Ark narrative, the day of YHWH's defeat at the hands
of the Philistines, is paralleled in the texts that precede and anticipate
2 Isaiah, verses that chronicle the evaporation of Israel's glory. Isaiah 10:1-
4, the final unit of the "woe series," anticipates a day of dreadful punishment, presumably at the hands of the Assyrians:[5]

What will you do on the day of punishment,
in the calamity that will come from far away?
To whom will you flee for help,
and where will you leave your *wealth*,
so as not to crouch among the prisoners
or fall among the slain?
For all this his anger has not turned away;
his hand is stretched out still. (Isa. 10:3-4)

The NRSV translates *kabod* as "wealth"; for our purposes it is enough that
the text anticipates the humiliation of Israel's *kabod*. In Isa. 17:3-4, the
coming humiliation of Damascus will match that of Israel:

3. There is no doubt that the *rereading* is designed for and serves principally Israel; but
because these textual rereadings have futures, what is given to Israel in a particular context
moves in rereading beyond Israel not only into Judaism but into Christianity and Islam as
well, and likely is generative even beyond those closely linked communities of rereading. A
classic case of such rereading is the work of Alfred Loisy, great Roman Catholic theologian,
on which see C. J. T. Talar, *(Re)Reading, Reception, and Rhetoric* (New York: Lang, 1999).

4. Appeal to "2 Isaiah" is, of course, increasingly problematic due to the ferment in the
critical and canonical study of the book of Isaiah. See the suggestive and representative discussions in *New Visions of Isaiah*, ed. Roy F. Melugin and Marvin A. Sweeney. JSOTSup 214
(Sheffield: Sheffield Academic, 1996); and *Writing and Reading the Scroll of Isaiah: Studies of
an Interpretive Tradition* 1 and 2, ed. Craig C. Broyles and Craig A. Evans. VTSup 70 (Leiden:
Brill, 1997). Nonetheless, the conventional nomenclature is useful as a shorthand reference
to that body of text.

5. On this series, see J. William Whedbee, *Isaiah & Wisdom* (Nashville: Abingdon,
1971), 80-110.

The remnant of Aram will be like the *glory* of the children of Israel,
says the Lord of hosts. (Isa. 17:3)

And then immediately:

On that day, the *glory* of Jacob will be brought low. (Isa. 17:4)

The same loss of glory is voiced in the book of Lamentations to which
2 Isaiah makes answer.[6] The loss, of course, is sweeping and thematic:

How lonely sits the city
that once was full of people!
How like a widow she has become,
she that was great among the nations!
She that was a princess among the provinces
has become a vassal. . . .
From daughter Zion has departed all her majesty *(hdr).*
Her princes have become like stags that find no pasture;
they fled without strength before the pursuer. . . .
Enemies have stretched out their hands
over all her precious things;
she has even seen the nations invade her sanctuary,
those whom you forbade to enter your congregation. . . .
How the Lord in his anger has humiliated daughter Zion!
He has thrown down from heaven to earth the splendor *(tp'rt)*
    of Israel;
he has not remembered his footstool in the day of his anger. . . .
He has bent his bow like an enemy,
with his right hand set like a foe;
he has killed all in whom we took pride
in the tent of daughter Zion;
he has poured out his fury like fire. . . .
The elders of daughter Zion sit on the ground in silence;
they have thrown dust on their heads and put on sackcloth;
the young girls of Jerusalem

6. On the large and generative force of the book of Lamentations, see Tod Linafelt, *Surviving Lamentations.*

125

have bowed their heads to the ground. . . .
All who pass along the way clap their hands at you;
they hiss and wag their heads
at daughter Jerusalem;
"Is this the city that was called the perfection of beauty,
the joy of all the earth?" (Lam. 1:1, 6, 10; 2:1, 4, 10, 15)

More specifically, the verdict on defeated Jerusalem from which
YHWH has departed sounds an echo of the Ark narrative:

He has made my teeth grind on gravel,
and made me cower in ashes;
my soul is bereft of peace;
I have forgotten what happiness is;
so I say, "Gone is my *glory*,
and all that I had hoped for from the Lord." (Lam. 3:16-18)

The phrasing in NRSV, "gone is my glory," sounds amazingly like the verdict of the wife of Phinehas:

The glory has departed from Israel. (1 Sam. 4:21)

In fact, the two phrases are very different. The Ark narrative uses *kabod*
with the verb *golah*, "exile"; the later poem uses *niṣaḥ* with the verb *'abad*.
It is not the same phrase; the point, however, is the same and Israel has
more than one way to speak of the same experience. In both cases, the desperate speech of loss is an acknowledgment that the force of YHWH that
has kept Israel's life buoyant is gone. Israel (Jerusalem) is bereft of resources, without hope, at risk, under threat. In both cases, differently said,
Israel voices the loss in all its depth, clear to the bottom, without ornamen-
tation or qualification.

The second day of the Ark narrative, the day of YHWH's recovery and
triumph, is more familiar to us in the cadences of 2 Isaiah. The "gospel
news" of 2 Isaiah, implied in the Ark narrative but never made explicit, is
the announcement that YHWH has defeated the Babylonian gods even as
Dagon was crushed in the night. The use of the term "gospel" (Isa. 40:9;
41:27; 52:7; NRSV "good tidings," "good news") and the humiliation of the

Babylonian gods in 46:1-2 are preparatory to the anticipated return of glory, still anticipated on the second day, even if now assured:[7]

> They shall see the glory of the Lord,
> the majesty of our God. . . .
> A highway shall be there,
> and it shall be called the Holy Way; . . .
> And the ransomed of the Lord shall return,
> and come to Zion with singing;
> everlasting joy shall be upon their heads;
> they shall obtain joy and gladness,
> and sorrow and sighing shall flee away. (Isa. 35:2, 8, 10)

And more familiarly:

> Every valley shall be lifted up,
> and every mountain and hill be made low;
> the uneven ground shall become level,
> and the rough places a plain.
> Then the *glory* of the Lord shall be revealed,
> and all people shall see it together,
> for the mouth of the Lord has spoken. (Isa. 40:4-5)

The second day anticipates a great triumphal return in splendor, glory visible not only to Israel, but to all nations, ready for the ransomed, the redeemed, the blind, the deaf, the lame, the speechless, all exuberant together (Isa. 35:8-10). We have already seen the new movement of *kabod* on the second day of the Ark narrative, and now the *kabod* moves victoriously home from exile, an exile already traced in the double use of *golah* in the Ark narrative (1 Sam. 4:21-22).

The third day is the triumphal procession home, the *kabod* now gathered and mobilized. In the Ark narrative, the triumphal procession is led by two willing milk cows who haul the ark toward Beth-shemesh in order to cross the boundary to Israel. YHWH travels on the ark, alone, but is received exuberantly by waiting Israel. In 2 Isaiah, the triumphal process is

---

7. On *baśar* in this exilic poetry, see Brueggemann, *Biblical Perspectives on Evangelism*, 14-47.

not YHWH alone, but now YHWH is accompanied on the glorious return by all the other exiles alongside this Chief Exile, all basking in the glory:

> Depart, depart, go out from there!
> Touch no unclean thing;
> go out from the midst of it,
> purify yourselves,
> you who carry the vessels of the Lord.
> For you shall not go out in haste,
> and you shall not go in flight,
> for the Lord will go before you,
> and the God of Israel will be your rear guard. (Isa. 52:11-12)

The return from Babylon — or from Ashdod — will be like the Exodus departure; but this time not in haste, this time with enough leisure to let the bread rise first. What a journey!

> For you shall go out in joy,
> and be led back in peace;
> the mountains and the hills before you
> shall burst into song,
> and all the trees of the field shall clap their hands. (Isa. 55:12)

Israel walks like a black church choir, singing, clapping, dancing, like Miriam's sisters (Exod. 15:20-21), joined in the doxology by hills and mountains and trees, all welcoming the emancipated homecoming of the Creator-King along with this community, welcoming the way they do the liturgical enthronement of YHWH (Ps. 96:11-12).

Of course, the parallels between old narrative and later poem are not precise and symmetrical. They are, however, close enough to see the three-day sequence:

> The utter defeat of glory;
> The stunning victory anticipated;
> The joyous journey back home.

In this three-day sequence, the peculiar tale of the Ashdod wonder is made into a script about *loss, exile,* and *homecoming.* The old primitive story is now taken up and *reread,* now a plot line for a deep crisis that no longer concerns the Philistines, but now concerns the Babylonians and their imperial gods. "For a brief moment" the gods of Babylon prevailed, and Israel sat by the rivers of Babylon and wept (Ps. 137:1; Isa. 54:7-8). But only for an instant, for the defeated, captured, impatient God of Israel has arisen and awakened to new life (see Isa. 51:9). As this God arises, so a buoyant future emerges for the people of this God, a future given in the drama of reassertion. It turns out that the Ark narrative is an inchoate characterization of the large and defining labor pains of emerging Judaism (see Isa. 42:14).

The inter-connection of Ark narrative and 2 Isaiah suggests a near-intentional rereading toward the defining drama of exile. If that connection is seen to be convincing, then I may suggest *a second rereading* that occurs alongside that of the Isaiah tradition. One might wonder why the Ark narrative is placed where it is in the so-called Deuteronomic history constituted, according to hypotheses, by the corpus of Judges through Kings. The Ark narrative is famous for having no human actors, but only the humiliated, triumphant God of the Ark. But of course in its present location, the Ark narrative is followed by the seeming failure of the old order under Samuel, and an argument about the monarchy (1 Sam. 7–15), the glad appearance of David (16:1-13) whose family turns immediately sordid and whose dynasty is filled with candidates like Millard Fillmore, Franklin Pierce, and Warren G. Harding, failures of spectacular proportion (2 Sam. 9–20, 1 Kgs. 1–2). The Ark narrative, in this larger literary embedment, is no longer about the ark. It is subsumed in the royal history, and it becomes a statement about that royal enterprise, about the fate of Jerusalem and the travail of Judah's life under the empire.

When it is recognized, as surely it must be, that 1 and 2 Kings are not a royal chronicle but in final form a meditation upon a failed dynasty, then we can see how the Ark narrative performs differently in fuller context. The royal history of Judean kings ends, famously, in 2 Kgs. 25:27-30 with Jehoiachin, the last king, recognized by the empire as a king under surveillance and house arrest, and so far as we know, without heirs or future (see Jer. 22:30). The ending is literarily one of great finesse, causing scholars to dispute about whether this is hope or a dread-filled termination.[8] Scholars

---

8. See Erich Zenger, "Die deuteronomistische Interpretation der Rehabilitierung Jojachins," *BZ* 12 (1968): 16-30; and the works cited there by Martin Noth, Hans Walter Wolff, and Gerhard von Rad.

must dispute because apparently, at that moment in the text, this narrator did not know what to say; he did not know what came next.[9]

Thus in a three-day sequence what we have in Kings is primarily a long telling of the first day. 2 Kings 25 tells of the defeat of Jerusalem and the sacking of the temple. The leading citizens are exiled, and all the temple equipment is carried away, though the ark is no longer mentioned.[10] YHWH has long since departed the city. The glory — theologically as YHWH's own presence, politically as the splendor of monarchy, liturgically as temple accoutrements — has long since departed. Perhaps the final paragraph in Kings (2 Kgs. 25:27-30) is a hint of the second day, the long stillness of exile without any home, so futile, because gone is "all that I had hoped for from the Lord" (Lam. 3:18). That is all the narrator can say, because that is all the narrator can see or know.

In this royal account, there is no third day. The third day is variously attested later on, but not by this narrative.[11] What a failure to have to end the narrative on the second day! But sometimes, candor requires: there is no third day. Except that the final form of the text has included the Ark narrative with all three days, including the third day of triumphal return. This third day claim, as we have seen, says no more than 2 Isaiah is able to say. What interests us, however, is that the Ark narrative is in the final form of the royal narrative.

Thus I suggest that the Ark narrative, embedded in the final form of the royal account, may be reread as a sketch of the whole of royal history. This narrative knows well about the first day that will indeed come upon the heirs of Josiah in all their ignominy. This narrative knows a little about the second day, the still, numbed waiting exile and not seeing yet. This narrative, amazingly, knows more about the third day of triumphal return than historical data will permit it to say.

Thus the third day of the glad sight at Beth-shemesh is a narrative told in anticipation, not yet grounded in "fact," but grounded deeper in the character of YHWH to which this narrative gives trusting attentiveness.

9. On not knowing what to say about what comes next, see Walter Brueggemann, "An Ending that Does not End" (forthcoming).

10. On the significance of the temple vessels for the depth of the ending of exile, see Peter R. Ackroyd, "The Temple Vessels: A Continuity Theme," *Studies in the Religion of Ancient Israel*. VTSup 23 (1972): 166-81.

11. This theme is picked up and advanced in 2 Chr. 36:22-23 in a way that goes beyond 2 Kings 25 and foresees the recovery after exile.

The third day, still awaited in the larger narrative of 2 Kings, is inchoately assured by this reread narrative. There will be a "heaviness" *(kabod)* enacted by the God of whom the empire has made light (see 1 Sam. 6:5). There will be a restoration, a homecoming, and an exaltation. Of this there is as yet no data; how does the narrative dare to say it, albeit under cover? Because the narrator knows more than the "facts" and does a rereading according to the surplus of conviction that does not wait for facts. The narrator knows the Ark narrative and the old Philistine tale. The narrator knows, moreover, that the old Philistine tale is shaped and informed by the older Egyptian tale of rescue. And out of these old memories, this narrator, with his community, has pieced together a conviction narratively rooted, but pressing beyond the available data:

> But this I call to mind,
> and therefore I have hope:
> The steadfast love of the Lord never ceases,
> his mercies never come to an end;
> they are new every morning;
> great is your faithfulness.
> "The Lord is my portion," says my soul,
> "therefore I will hope in him." (Lam. 3:21-24)

This is, to be sure, hope beyond fact and beyond circumstance. It is hope that points to the nadir of exile, that denies nothing of exile, except that exile is the termination of YHWH's glory. This rereading takes the royal chronicle fully into account, but knows that the future of YHWH is not contained in the shabbiness of David's family or in the pitiful performance of Josiah's heirs. I propose then that the Ark narrative is in its present location precisely to force a *rereading* in faith of the royal account and almost, inadvertently, to provide a plot sketch for the story beyond Jehoiachin. With the reading toward exilic Isaiah and Kings exiled, the Ark narrative draws all of our attention to the depth of exile, the same exile to which the Ark had descended in Ashdod. The narrative denies nothing, but knows as well about the arousal of *kabod*. The frightened, bewildered response of the Philistines to YHWH's aroused *kabod* is the script for all those who think they will defeat the God of Israel (1 Sam. 5:7, 11; 6:2). They may gloat . . . briefly. For Israel, it is true that

weeping may linger for the night,
but joy comes with the morning (Ps. 30:5).

The third day, the day that in Israel is beyond the scope of the royal chronicle, is given only in narrative and dancing doxology.

V

I now move in a great leap to a third *rereading* that you have by now anticipated. In the German-American church community in which I grew up, we were nurtured on what was called "The Catechism," properly *The Evangelical Catechism,* a derivative from Luther's *Smaller Catechism* and the *Heidelberg Catechism,* with all of the cadences of Reformation theological claim. When it came time for "examination" before the congregation, anxiety concerned who would be asked the dreaded question #72. I got it on that day, because my father was the pastor and he had schooled me well. The question is:

Wherein is the humiliation and exaltation of Christ briefly expressed?

The only part of the question and answer not now convincing to me is that word "briefly." The answer is:

The humiliation and exaltation of Christ is briefly expressed in Phil. 2:5-11, which is as follows:

Let the same mind be in you that was in Christ Jesus,
who, though he was in the form of God,
did not regard equality with God as something to be exploited,
but emptied himself,
taking the form of a slave,
being born in the human likeness.
And being found in human form,
he humbled himself
and became obedient to the point of death —
even death on a cross.

Therefore God also highly exalted him
and gave him the name that is above every name,
so that at the name of Jesus
every knee should bend,
in heaven and on earth and under the earth,
and every tongue should confess that Jesus Christ is Lord,
to the glory of God the Father.

I answered the question that day of confirmation examination. Of course, I answered far more than I even suspected that day. But then, whenever we cite that text, we say more than we know. I did not know then that this text is the primary plot text for the gospel narrative, that the early hymn provided the hints for all subsequent claims and disputes about Trinitarian doctrine. I thought then that it was a text chosen by the catechism people who could have chosen otherwise, but who did this one at random.

But of course they could hardly have chosen otherwise, and in any case, they did not. They did not choose otherwise because in this pre-Pauline hymn everything is present concerning "pre-existent" equality with God before all time, the risky descent into human form and human obedience, and the ultimate exaltation, an exaltation before which every knee shall bow and every tongue confess, a cadence not possible without the intertextuality of Isa. 45:23. There is everything here about the pivot of Friday before the authorities and the jarring of Sunday about which the authorities are able to speak not at all. There is here the outline of the soon-to-come creed:

... Suffered under Pontius Pilate, was crucified, dead, and buried. He descended into hell. The third day he rose again from the dead. He ascended into heaven, and sitteth on the right hand of God the Father Almighty.

This hymn moves so deftly from gospel reportage to creedal fugue that we hardly notice what is accomplished. All of this the makers of *The Evangelical Catechism* and my father knew fully.

But my father, educated as he was in historical criticism, did not know, except intuitively, about intertextuality and rereading. We can see more clearly now with better method what he and they understood intuitively, that the life and destiny of Jesus, as given us lyrically, is a rereading and reliving and re-enacting of Israel's decisive experience in the world.[12] The pre-Pauline hymn is indeed something very like a three-day sequence behind which stands, among other memories, the drama of Ashdod:

Day one: he became obedient unto death, even death on a cross . . . not unlike the deathly scene before Dagon at Ashdod.

Day two: In the hymn of Philippians 2, the matter is the open, "empty" [sic] space between verse 8 and verse 9. In the NRSV, it is a considerable space, allowing for an entire day to pass, a night and a day of stillness when the outcome is not yet visible, when YHWH is gathering the energies of *kabod* for a final assertion.

Day three: Therefore exalted,
Therefore seen in glory,
Therefore welcomed by the peasants at Beth-shemesh,
Therefore on the way rejoicing.

The pre-Pauline hymn will make its own statement that is, of course, adequate on its own. But to read such a cadence only as its own statement is to miss the thickness that Paul would surely have understood. Faithful as the hymn is to the canonical life of Jesus, it is also a deep and massive *re-reading* of old texts in which the church is embedded. When the church sings of this three-day wonder that redefines the world and gives to the church its ethic of alterity, the church,

- resings 2 Isaiah about the departure of glory and the gospel of the return of glory;
- resings the royal tale of failed kings that comes to stillness in Jehoiachin and waits;
- resings the Ark narrative with its shrill defeat, its homeward triumph, and finally even Philistine affirmation of YHWH.
- With careful listening, moreover, one can hear, just as background music in Ashdod, Miriam and her sisters singing about the God of the slaves now come to power.

---

12. N. T. Wright, *Christian Origins and the Question of God,* 1: *The New Testament and the People of God* (Minneapolis: Fortress, 1992), has gone far in developing his Christology in this direction.

The several dramatic tellings are not to be reduced, homogenized, or made generic. Each retelling and resinging is on its own, each one concretely and historically located. They call out to each other and illuminate each other; they invite not the monologic but the symphonic, and they drive the reciting community far away from the three-day void of weekend to this three-day decision,

- against denial for truth-telling,
- against despair for buoyancy,
- against complacency to attentiveness.

As we move from the *three-day void* of weekend to the *three-day drama* of faith, a different community is formed, a different vision is evoked, and a different ethic is made possible. To be sure, I have not pushed the drama to ethics, because the Ark narrative itself does not explicitly go there. But one can easily and legitimately voice the next ethical claim:

- No doubt the Ark narrative, minded by Samuel, has in mind the *ethic of Deuteronomy;* for in 1 Sam. 8:11-17, two chapters later, this same Samuel warns against a rapacious injustice, and in 1 Samuel 12 he champions torah obedience.
- No doubt 2 Isaiah's gospel has close at hand *the ethic of 3 Isaiah,* its cadences of inclusiveness without reference to ethnicity or sexual condition (Isa. 56) and its solidarity with the poor and marginated (Isa. 58).
- And surely Paul in his great hymn, deals with real ecclesial conflict:

If then there is any encouragement in Christ, any consolation from love, any sharing in the Spirit, any compassion and sympathy, make my joy complete: be of the same mind, having the same love, being in full accord and of one mind. Do nothing from selfish ambition or conceit, but in humility regard others as better than yourselves. Let each of you look not to your own interests, but to the interests of others. (Phil. 2:1-4)

What a claim: regard others as better! Look to the interests of others, stunning mandate across the lines of rich and poor, black and white, male and female, North and South, Amendments A and B. How far *Deuteron-*

omy on the year of release to widow, orphan, and alien? How far 3 Isaiah on inclusiveness and solidarity? How far with *Paul* can one look to the interests of others? How far all of that is from the ethic-less ideology of the weekend! In the telling, the retelling, and the rereading, and the resinging, a different community is formed, a different transformative ethic is fashioned that is marked by truth-telling, buoyancy, and attentiveness. My question about what the church does before a text . . . by way of *nonfoundationalism, intertextuality,* and *rereading* . . . is answered that through the text the church submits to a different rhetoric that carries a different world. Before the text and its rereading, this community, as drop-out from the ideology of weekend, is formed and reformed and formed again, texted by a countertext, suited for guerilla theater.[13]

VI

By my rereading and by my sense of dramatic sequence, dramatic development, and dramatic coherence, I am led to consider the three-day mystery of Friday-Saturday-Sunday, what Hans Urs von Balthasar terms *The Paschale Mystery: The Mystery of Easter.*[14] In speaking of this mystery, the evangelical *triduum,* von Balthasar focuses on the kenosis, the emptying, the eternal, super-kenosis, the abysslike depths of the Father's self-giving in which is hidden all the truth of God's life in the world and God's will for the world. He begins, of course, with the hymn of Philippians 2. Of that affirmation, he writes that the church, in patristic reading,

> went on to see in the powerlessness of the Incarnate and Crucified One the shining forth of God's *omnipotence.*[15]

He quotes Gregory of Nyssa with approval:

13. On text-based counteractivity as a way to develop community, see William T. Cavanaugh, *Torture and Eucharist: Theology, Politics, and the Body of Christ* (Oxford: Blackwell, 1998). The celebration of Eucharist in the Chilean context Cavanaugh describes assures that the sacrament is indeed a guerilla activity, with all the characteristic risks and potential of such action.

14. Hans Urs von Balthasar, *Mysterium Paschale: The Mystery of Easter* (Grand Rapids: Wm. B. Eerdmans, 1990).

15. Von Balthasar, *Mysterium Paschale,* 34.

The humiliation of God shows the super-abundance of his power, which is in no way fettered in the midst of conditions contrary to its nature. . . . The greatness is glimpsed in the lowliness and its exaltation is not thereby reduced.[16]

Von Balthasar himself continues after Gregory:

There is a theological truth which mediates between the two irreconcilable extremes: those of, on the one hand, a 'divine immutability' for which the Incarnation appears only as an external 'addition', and, on the other a 'divine mutability' of such a sort that, for the duration of the Incarnation, the divine self-consciousness of the Son is 'alienated' in a human awareness.[17]

I shall not follow von Balthasar in his argument very far, because his way of thinking as a dogmatician, made more complex by the assumptions of his Roman Catholic philosophical project, is more esoteric than I can fathom. Beyond that, however, is the fact that his mystical categories lead away from the earthly, political, material reality that properly belongs to the story of this God. It is enough to notice that he is able to write 32 pages on "Going to the Dead: Holy Saturday" that culminates with his topic, "Salvation in the Abyss."[18] Of that Saturday so dreadfully placed between Friday and Sunday, he writes:

We must, in the first place, guard against that theological busyness and religious impatience which insist on anticipating the moment of fruiting of the eternal redemption through the temporal passion — on dragging forward that moment from Easter to Holy Saturday.[19]

In other words, let Saturday be Saturday, and do not let Sunday seep over into it in order to claim an early victory, a temptation perhaps of some Easter vigils. This is exactly the restraint practiced by our narrator in 1 Samuel 4. He too makes us wait until dawn.

16. Von Balthasar, *Mysterium Paschale*, 34.
17. Von Balthasar, *Mysterium Paschale*, 34.
18. Von Balthasar, *Mysterium Paschale*, esp. 176-81.
19. Von Balthasar, *Mysterium Paschale*, 179.

In the superabundant self-giving of God, Friday, Saturday, and Sunday are distinct days as the three days already are dramatically and theologically distinct in Ashdod. Saturday, in that narrative, is that dark, still unuttered moment between chapter 4 and chapter 5, left so much in poverty that it does not even come to text. In that still, dark instant, Dagon perhaps still smirks and YHWH still twists in pain, and the church pauses in its reading, content not to rush to the "rumble" of chapter 5, content to let the sounds of YHWH's degradation echo and re-echo and have their say, while the muscles are flexed to make the loss into a victory for other exiles.

On the same theme of the *triduum,* we move out of von Balthasar's mystical categories into the harshness of lived life by the conclusion of George Steiner. The contrast of style and mode of expression from the Roman Catholic mystic and this Jewish academic are stunning. I have quoted Steiner often before, but he bears hearing yet again, because his is an elegant piece of theological pondering:

There is one particular day in Western history about which neither historical record nor myth nor Scripture make report. It is a Saturday. And it has become the longest of days. We know of that Good Friday which Christianity holds to have been that of the Cross. But the non-Christian, the atheist, knows of it as well. This is to say that he knows of the injustice, of the interminable suffering, of the waste, of the brute enigma of ending, which so largely make up not only the historical dimension of the human condition, but the everyday fabric of our personal lives. We know, ineluctably, of the pain, of the failure of love, of the solitude which are our history and private fate. We know also about Sunday. To the Christian, that day signifies an intimation, both assured and precarious, both evident and beyond comprehension, of resurrection, of a justice and a love that have conquered death. If we are non-Christians or non-believers, we know of that Sunday in precisely analogous terms. We conceive of it as the day of liberation from inhumanity and servitude. We look to resolutions, be they therapeutic or political, be they social or messianic. The lineaments of that Sunday carry the name of hope (there is no word less deconstructible).

But ours is the long day's journey of the Saturday. Between suffering, aloneness, unutterable waste on the one hand and the dream of liberation, of rebirth on the other. In the face of the torture of a child, of the death of love which is Friday, even the greatest art and poetry are almost helpless. In the Utopia of the Sunday, the aesthetic will, presumably, no longer have logic or necessity. The apprehensions and figurations in the play of metaphysical imagining, in the poem and the music, which tell of pain and of hope, of the flesh which is said to taste of ash and of the spirit which is said to have the savour of fire, are always Sabbatarian. They have risen out of an immensity of waiting which is that of man. Without them, how could we be patient?[20]

The move from von Balthasar to Steiner is, of course, immense. And perhaps Christians will not fully resonate with this Jewish statement that only hopes and has not yet seen, and that seems to settle finally for an aesthetic possibility at best.

Acknowledging all of that, however, we learn from and stand with this Jew Steiner in the deep awareness that Saturday is very long indeed. Of course, any Jew who writes of the "taste of ash" is forever near to Auschwitz; but then, the Saturday is more than long enough in many other places, the spectacular places we name such as Kosovo and the Gaza Strip and Soweto. But the day is not much shorter in our inner cities and in the unbearable marriages and cancer diagnoses where every pastor spends hard days. The pause in Philippians 2 between "obedient to the point of death" (v. 8) and "therefore God highly exalted" (v. 9) required a second day that was long but not dramatic. The gap in Ashdod between "Ichabod" and *kabod*, between chapter 4 and chapter 5, moreover, is immense, as immense as the Rivers of Babylon and Jehoiachin's daily royal meal under imperial surveillance. Immense indeed, the scene where our future emerges out of Saturday if it emerges out of anywhere, out of Saturday, that forlorn but haunted place of God's own residence.

The acknowledgment of the long Saturday — bounded by the vulnerability of Friday and the victory of Sunday, bounded by the capture of the ark and the return of the ark, bounded by the destruction of Jerusalem and its re-emergence in Judaism, bounded by the departure of glory and the reappearance of glory in changed form — that Saturday runs dead against the consumer glory of the weekend. The three days that pivot on Saturday

20. George Steiner, *Real Presences* (Chicago: University of Chicago Press, 1989), 231-32.

break the weekend passion for entertainment rooted in denial and numbness rooted in despair. The God whom we confess in the story of Jesus "suffered under Pontius Pilate, died, and was buried on Friday and on the third day rose again on Sunday" is crucially a Saturday God who descended and descends yet again into hell. That is what happened in Ashdod and in Babylon and in Philippi.

When the church and its preachers stand before this text and the host of texts with which this one makes intimate contact, it is characteristically that Saturday dimension of this God of Israel that stands at the center of the dramatic retelling. We do not do much theology or liturgy about that Saturday; but every pastor knows, because the church and its pastors are exactly Saturday people, pressed taut between Friday and Sunday wherever the glory has departed. I say whenever the glory has departed — in Ashdod or Jerusalem or Kosovo or the Congo or the inner city of Atlanta or Aunt Helen's cancer or Lockerbie or Columbine or a host of other places that are in your heart this day. The weekend permits simply a turn of the channel to a happier sit-com or a more interesting match; but this *triduum* we confess and retell is no sit-com and no "test match," but death-or-life. There is this Saturday wait, this inescapable, always demanding Saturday wait until the next morning, early the next morning, a wait for joy that comes in the morning, a wait until mourning is turned to dancing and sackcloth is displaced by joy, a long wait, a wait of candor.

It is this wait, this caesura, that marks evangelical faith as much as the victory, and that sets this texted community apart from the weekend deception. Whereas weekend thins, this *triduum* yields all the imaginable thickness of humanness given as gift, task, and burden by this God who calls all things into existence, even at Beth-shemesh (Rom. 4:17), and who brings to nought the things that are, even at Ashdod (1 Cor. 1:28). The intransigence and unyielding quality of the wait, so clear at Ashdod in that time past, has yielded newness. The next morning, the smirk is wiped away from the face of Dagon and the "heaviness" heads home.

It turns out, in my judgment, that the Ark narrative is indeed a very large subject, the kind Professor Anderson has insisted upon. I have asked, what does the church do when it stands before the text. I have suggested four facets of that standing before that belong to the pastoral practice of the church:

1. A *nonfoundational* readiness to "follow" the text in all its oddness, in

an exercise of imagination uncurbed by the old safe readings of "history," "reason" or "canon."[21]

2. An *intertextual* attentiveness that discovers that this text sends out lines and lineaments to many other texts, many other scenarios, some Jewish, some Christian, some exilic, some late, where the odd evangelical claims of the text are traced in various ways with inexhaustible freshness of imagination. The intertextual requires us to have all the texts in purview, not just the ones we like, not just the ones familiar, in order to read any one text well.

3. A *rereading* after the locus of Ashdod and Dagon and the Philistines, to notice that the text is about Ashdod and *many other* places, about Dagon and *many other* gods, about the Philistines and *many other* peoples, about the rout of the ark and *many other* defeats, about the surprise of the third day and *many other* surprises, about the still night and *many other* Saturdays, each of which is like all the others and each of which is unique to itself alone, requiring our full and uncompromised attention. Circumstance does indeed push and pull, twist and insist on holding the text close to the lived reality of our present moment that defines all else. This texted community does not shrink from bold rereading, to depart from Ashdod and to come to a new place, the old place yet again, where we have never been before. Or we may say with Eliot:

> We shall not cease from exploration
> and the end of all our exploring
> will be to arrive where we started
> and know the place for the first time.[22]

That, is it not, is what happens in our endless rereading.

4. Implicit in this final lecture is a fourth facet of our reading. After we attend to the vexed issue of "historicity" in which we are so well schooled, we notice in our rereading that we and our life have been *decisively reread* in the process of rereading the text. We have been reread away from the denial and the despair of the weekend, into all the thickness of a brooding,

---

21. On the capacity to "follow" a narrative text, see W. B. Gallie, "The Historical Understanding."

22. T. S. Eliot, "Little Gidding," *The Complete Poems and Plays 1909-1950* (New York: Harcourt, Brace, and World, 1962), 145.

waiting Saturday that gathers all Friday suffering and moves toward all the Sunday glory come again. We find in being reread we have been *rescripted* for a different life in the world.

This rereading I take to be urgent in our weekend society where human questions are muted and forfeited in our oceans of commodity. That is why, for all its increasing marginality in our society — or perhaps precisely in its marginality — the church, its texts, and its pastors are pivotal for the future. The critical issue is not the survival of the church in a secular society; it is rather the honest and full acknowledgment of "Ichabod" and the deep joy of *kabod* en route home in joy. It is clear among us, is it not, that this script for rescripting matters decisively, for it is this scripting that gives us the Friday-Saturday-Sunday Character without whom there is no serious future and no reliable present.

Having said *nonfoundational, intertextual, rereading,* and *being reread,* I am finished. Except for one other incidental notice. At the end of 1 Samuel 4, that terrible Friday of failure, Eli's unnamed daughter-in-law, wife of Phinehas, bears a son. The mother is about to die; she endures in the narrative only long enough to name her son, rendered by P. Kyle McCarter, "Alas for the glory!"[23] This little son, never heard from again, is seldom noticed in the narrative and rarely commented upon. His obvious function in the narrative is to assure that the utterance "Ichabod" will be sounded as his name in the text, and then his narrative function is completed.

Except that this text and its attentive readers always pay attention when a son is born (see, e.g., Isa. 9:6). For a son means that there is yet a future. As in the ancestral narratives of Genesis, here the son means that the family of Eli is not yet terminated. There is a future. The prayer book says, "While we live, we are in the presence of death." But here the narrative counterasserts: "While we die, we are in the presence of new life." It is likely that this birth account is a "type-scene," a recurring narrative pattern of midwives encouraging a mother in labor.[24] So in Gen. 35:17 at the birth of Benjamin, the midwives assure Rachel:

Do not be afraid; for now you will have another son.

---

23. P. Kyle McCarter, Jr., *I Samuel.* AB 8 (Garden City: Doubleday, 1980), 116.

24. On "type-scenes," see Robert Alter, *The Art of Biblical Narrative* (New York: Basic Books, 1981), 47-62.

And in Ruth, the midwives say to Naomi of Ruth's baby:

"Blessed be the Lord, who has not left you this day without next-of-kin; and may his name be remembered in Israel." . . . The women of the neighborhood gave him a name, saying, "A son has been born to Naomi." They named him Obed; he became the father of Jesse, the father of David. (Ruth 4:14-17)

Benjamin and finally David . . . not bad company for little "Ichabod"! The parallels suggest this little son is more important than appears at first glance, because a son is a harbinger for a future God will give, a hint across the abyss of Saturday in Ashdod.

This community, always up against it on Friday, pays attention to the new child. It was so with barren Sarah and barren Rebekah and barren Rachel and barren Hannah and barren Elizabeth. There are enough dreadful memories of barrenness in Israel that in exile the poet could take up the theme on that long Saturday of displacement:

Sing, O barren one who did not bear;
burst into song and shout,
you who have not been in labor!
For the children of the desolate woman will be more
than the children of her that is married, says the Lord.
Enlarge the site of your tent,
and let the curtains of your habitations be stretched out;
do not hold back; lengthen your cords
and strengthen your stakes.
For you will spread out to the right and to the left,
and your descendants will possess the nations
and will settle the desolate towns. (Isa. 54:1-3)

The imagery of teeming children means for the poet that the long Saturday of Babylon will soon be over.

As you know, moreover, Paul finds this imagery of barrenness to birth a way to speak about the extravagance of grace to "the free woman":

Rejoice, you childless one, you who bear no children,
burst into song and shout,

143

you who endure no birthpangs;
for the children of the desolate woman are more numerous
than the children of the one who is married. (Gal. 4:27)

The little son born at the last moment to the family of Eli is an inexplicable assurance of the future, even while the glory is gone. It is, moreover,
all made possible by these midwives who encourage and assure, "do not
fear."[25] The midwives who encourage Rachel with "do not fear" (Gen.
35:17) are the same women who celebrate with Ruth (Ruth 4:14-17); they
belong to a long history of midwives who keep waiting in hope. At their
head are Siphrah and Puah, who "feared God" and refused imperial brutality (Exod. 1:15-22). As in Egypt, so at Ashdod, the midwives refused
Philistine definitions of reality, refused to accept the departure of glory as
the end of the matter, hoped right through the abyss with this fragile gift of
the son. The narrative leaves us wondering and does not tell us,

What child is this?

The question lingers in the community of those three days of extremity
where nothing is as thin and obvious as we had thought. The community
in this narrative still asks:

What child is this?

Even when we move from this unnamed woman to that scandalous
mother in Bethlehem, the question persists and the church is haunted by
the echo yet:

What child is this?

What child indeed?
So to finish. It is the *triduum* with its Saturday pivot that breaks the
weekend ideology of death. This Saturday accent may cause some of you to
ask:

25. See Edgar W. Conrad, *Fear Not Warrior: A Study of 'al tîrā' Pericopes in the Hebrew
Scriptures.* BJS 75 (Chico: Scholars, 1985), 160, n. 3; and the more complete theological exposition of Patrick D. Miller, *They Cried to the Lord,* 135-77.

Does this reading take the redemption of Friday seriously enough? And I answer with sadness, "Yes."

Does this reading take the victory of Sunday exuberantly enough? And I answer with joy, "Yes."

But the church in its concrete, daily life of praise and obedience knows about the durability of Saturday that the weekend crowd will not notice. We wait with memory; we wait with hope; but we wait . . . at the gap between tears and laughter.

For those of you worried yet about history, reason, or canon, I will give the penultimate word to that Irish novelist Alice McDermott, who concludes her tale of "Charming Billy" this way in commenting on the hidden women of her narrative, as hidden as the daughter in-law in our account:

> Some doubt had arisen about whether or not she had actually lived. As if, in that wide-ranging anthology of stories that was the lives of the saints — that was as well, my father's faith and Billy's and some part of my own — what was actual, as opposed to what was imagined, as opposed to what was believed, made, when you got right down to it, any difference at all.[26]

And now the ultimate word for the day to that Irish poet Seamus Heaney, in his comment on another bold woman, this one named Nadezhda Mandelstam:

26. Alice McDermott, *Charming Billy* (New York: Random House, 1998), 242-43. In a very different context, Frank Moore Cross, *From Epic to Canon: History and Literature in Ancient Israel* (Baltimore: Johns Hopkins University Press, 1998), 28, considers how to label such strange material as we have on our hands in the Bible:

The term *fiction* is chosen to point to the nonhistorical features of the narrative, presumably, but it suggests that the composer of Israelite traditional narrative chose to "write" what would look like historiography, but composed fiction in such a guise. I do not believe his intent was to compose history, or to compose "fiction," or to compose one under the guise of the other. I believe he was seeking to sing of Israel's past using traditional themes, the common stuff of generations of singers and tellers of tales. His story, prose or poetry. . ., dealt with the interactions of Yahweh and Israel in the normative past. The historian, even one given to fictionalizing, does not make a deity his main character. The creator of fiction who wishes "to move away from the world of myth" does not make free use of such mythic themes in shaping his "historicized fiction." The term *fiction*, like *history*, is anachronistic when applied to Israel's national story, and derives — to use Ivan Engnell's strong language — from an arrogant *interpretatio europaeica moderna*.

Suddenly she became a guerrilla of the imagination. . . . From then on, she was like a hunted priest in penal times, travelling danger- ously with the altar-stone of the forbidden faith, disposing the manuscripts for safe keeping among the secret adherents. And inev- itably, having considered herself a guardian, she was destined to be- come a witness.[27]

The echo of Amos Wilder in Seamus Heaney strikes me; all of us in our life of faith are destined to be witnesses, depositing the manuscripts, "guerrillas of the imagination." Imagine Sunday morning or any text time, imagine the pastor left holding this dangerous, hidden script. And then running across the sanctuary, running across the stadium in Bucharest, filled with people agape. The strutting entourage of Nicolae Ceausescu, the "weekend crowd" expecting nothing new. The banner is unfurled; the hid- den script is gone public; the crowd laughs an Easter laugh at the pretense of the weekend of consumerism. The crowd cheers in deep places long de- nied. The crowd cries in pain long covered by despair. For the banner says, all over the text, "Friday-Saturday-Sunday." The truth is told. The timeless regime is mocked to nullity. It is now known, perhaps for the first time, what time it is, time of suffering, time of joy, time of waiting. There is no one else to fling wide the banner of the actual, the imagined, the believed. No one else, except this newly born child . . . and us.

27. Seamus Heaney, *The Government of the Tongue: The 1986 T. S. Eliot Memorial Lec- tures and Other Critical Writings* (London: Faber and Faber, 1988), 73.

Index of Scripture References